BRENDAN
BEHAN'S
NEW YORK

By Brendan Behan

Borstal Boy
Brendan Behan's Island (with Paul Hogarth)
Hold Your Hour and Have Another
(with decorations by Beatrice Behan)

PLAYS

The Quare Fellow
The Hostage
The Big House

By Paul Hogarth

Defiant People: Drawings of Greece Today
Looking at China
The Face of Europe
People Like Us
Brendan Behan's Island (with Brendan Behan)
Creative Pencil Drawing
Majorca Observed (with Robert Graves)
London à la Mode (with Malcolm Muggeridge)
Artist as Reporter
Russian Journey (with A. Jacob)
Drawing People
Artists on Horseback
Drawing Architecture
Paul Hogarth's American Album
Creative Ink Drawing
Walking Tours of Old Philadelphia
Walking Tours of Old Boston
America Observed (with Stephen Spender)
Arthur Boyd Houghton

GREENWICH VILLAGE:
The WASHINGTON ARCH, WASHINGTON SQ

BRENDAN BEHAN'S NEW YORK

by
BRENDAN BEHAN

with drawings by
PAUL HOGARTH

HUTCHINSON
London Melbourne Sydney Auckland Johannesburg

Hutchinson & Co. (Publishers) Ltd

An imprint of the Hutchinson Publishing Group

17-21 Conway Street, London W1P 6JD

Hutchinson Group (Australia) Pty Ltd
30-32 Cremorne Street, Richmond South, Victoria 3121
PO Box 151, Broadway, New South Wales 2007

Hutchinson Group (NZ) Ltd
32-34 View Road, PO Box 40-086, Glenfield, Auckland 10

Hutchinson Group (SA) Pty Ltd
PO Box 337, Bergvlei 2012, South Africa

First published 1964
First published as a Hutchinson Paperback 1984
© Beatrice Behan and Paul Hogarth 1964

British Library Cataloguing in Publication Data
Behan, Brendan
    Brendan Behan's New York.
    1. New York (N.Y.) – Description–1951–
    I. Title   II. Hogarth, Paul
    917.47′10443   F128.52

Printed and bound in Great Britain by Anchor Brendon Ltd,
Tiptree, Essex

ISBN 0 09 155871 9

Contents

The F.B.I.
comes to Town
page 11

What are they at
round Broadway
and the bars?
page 39

Down-Town
Up-Town and
in and out of
Harlem
page 77

Beats, Boweryites
and Chinamen
page 113

Give my regards
to Staten Island
page 141

TO AMERICA
MY NEW-FOUND LAND.
THE MAN THAT HATES YOU
HATES THE HUMAN RACE.

Bay Ridge Cemetery, Brooklyn

The F.B.I.
comes to Town

I am the child of the King of Greece's son
          who married the King of Ireland's daughter,
          and travelled west.
The Red Sea opened for us. We were quakers before God,
          but quaked before no earthly King.
We are people of the Bible,
          Old Testament,
          New Testament,
          or no Testament.
We carried Los Angeles with us,
          and Luther and Francis of Assisi
          and Robert Ingersoll and Tom Paine.
We are white, coffee coloured, black and beautiful bronze.
We are as painful as human life and as exciting.
We are men.
Birds, we are told at school, where the lessons are
          obviously slanted by crypto-bird teachers,
          are very clever and build nests.
But how many birds would it take
          to build the Empire State Building?

'New York City is hell,' said an old Midwest lady who was living with me at the Algonquin Hotel. She had a room on the same floor and used the lift with us, that is.

'I never felt so much at home anywhere as I do in New York,' I answered.

'That could very well be,' said the old Midwest lady.

I am not afraid to admit that New York is the greatest city on the face of God's earth. You only have to look at it, from the air, from the river, from Father Duffy's statue. New York is easily recognizable as the greatest city in the world, view it any way and every way – back, belly and sides.

London is a wide flat pie of redbrick suburbs with the West End stuck in the middle like a currant. New York is a huge rich raisin and is the biggest city I can imagine.

A city is a place where Man lives, walks about, talks and eats and drinks in the bright light of day or electricity for twenty-four hours a day. In New York, at three o'clock in the morning, you can walk about, see crowds, read the papers and have a drink – orange juice, coffee, whiskey or anything. It is the greatest show on earth, for everyone. Its fabulous beauty at night, even forty years ago, was the wonder of the world.

When I arrived home from Broadway, where my play *The Hostage* was running, my wife said to me, 'Oh isn't it great to be back. How do you feel coming home?'

'Listen Beatrice,' I said, 'It's very dark!'

And I think anybody returning home after going to New York will find their native spot pretty dark too.

We don't come to a city to be alone, and the test of a city is the ease with which you can see and talk to other people. A city is a place where you are least likely to get a bite from a wild sheep and I'd say that New York is the friendliest city I know. The young Russian poet, Yevtushenko, said that in all honesty he had to admit that New York was the most exciting place that he had ever been to in his entire life.

I knew an old Irishman who went there when he was seventy-five and ill, and like a Lourdes of light, New York cured him and he lived for years afterwards, a healthy and happy old man. He painted my wife's grandmother and his name was Jack Yeats, the father of William Butler Yeats, the great poet of Ireland and the world, and Jack B. Yeats, a great painter himself.

My wife says New York is like a fancy fair and the person who says that he's not impressed by the skyline, he's either half blind or he's just simply a liar.

One of the most amazing things I discovered about the Americans, and the New Yorkers in particular, is the way in which they are always boasting about bribery and corruption, as if it was their own special invention and as if nobody else had any. They boast of the heartlessness of the multitude and how a man could lie in Times Square for a month without anyone going near him, except it was to rob him or rape him. I think they have, like the rest of us, seen too many films about New York, and of course, they are paying themselves the compliment by describing the wickedness of that great city and what big bad wolves they must be, to survive in it. What a tough town it is. What a tough guy he is to have lived so many years in it. The melting pot of the world, and he was born there.

If you were to tell a New Yorker that he is not the most fast man in the world after the dollar, well, he'd be kind of insulted, but he's also pretty good at giving it away. Despite wise guys telling about bums dying with millions of money, I have never met anyone who already had a dime asking a stranger in the street for one. Nobody asks for money who doesn't genuinely need it. It's like saying you've got a personal friend. If you have a friend, he's a friend. How the hell can he be otherwise than a personal friend?

I had lunch once with the District Attorney of New York, Frank S. Hogan, and I talked about crime in the city. Now my knowledge of district attorneys is not very great, as the only other one I know is Bernie Hoffer who is a very strong Zionist. He sent his wife and family, who came from New York, over to Israel to do agricultural work and I think, much as they were fond of Israel, they were not exactly cut out for agricultural activity and they found it easier to get by on Manhattan.

However, Frank Hogan seemed to me to be a very humane individual and he explained to me that a great deal of crime on the part of the teenagers, which happens everywhere, is due to a variety of reasons. In some cases, he said, it was the parents' fault and in others, it was due to the economic conditions. He did not blame any particular race or creed, but it is obvious that the newer immigrants are

GANG BOYS, LOWER EAST SIDE

not economically very well off. I hate the word underprivileged, but I could see that the high rate of crime amongst these youngsters is not altogether the kids' fault.

I don't think Frank Hogan relished talking very much about having to prosecute people who were sometimes sent to the electric chair, so we began to talk about more pleasant things.

'Brendan,' he said, 'a lot of Irish people tell me that my mother wasn't Irish because she didn't have an Irish name.'

'Before you go any further,' I interrupted him, 'I will tell you, first of all, that her name was Smithwick, pronounced in Ireland, "Smithick" and secondly, that I have met your cousin, Walter Smithwick, a brewer with whom I have enjoyed several excellent ales, and furthermore,' I said, 'I can tell you that he lives on an estate in Kilkenny, in a house called Kilcreene Lodge and that in his home, amongst other things, he has a lifesize painting of Napoleon by Jacques Louis David, the famous French painter of the Revolution and of the Napoleonic Court.'

DISCOS DISCOS

CASA MICHAEL
DISCOS

"The ASSASSINS"

'It is you who should be District Attorney,' said Frank Hogan. 'You seem to know everything.'

I was in a little bit of trouble myself once, north of the border, up in Canada, which may or may not have been my fault. I am not trying to give Canada a boost I can tell you, despite the fact that if any Canadian is a cash customer and buys this book, he has got my blessing. But Toronto will be a fine place when it is finished.

The late Gilbert Harding, who was a well known English television personality, was up in Toronto one time with the Canadian Broadcasting Corporation, and he was asked by a society hostess where he was staying in Toronto. When he told her the address, she said: 'That's not a very good address, Mr. Harding.'

'No,' said Gilbert Harding, 'neither is Toronto.'

I was allowed out for a week on a thousand dollar bail and I wanted to spend it somewhere not very far from Times Square. The man who bailed me out told me that he would like to come down to New York for a visit, but was impertinent enough to say that he would not like to stay there. I am sure that a lot of my readers would express the same sentiment. My reply to one and all is:

'Well, who sent for you?'

A quarter of a million people arrive there each year so I don't think New York will be running short of residents just yet.

The taxis in New York are very inexpensive compared with any other city I have been in and they are always around the place. The taxi drivers try to live up to the reputation that all taxi drivers have, of being a wit. As I am in the wit line myself, I object to competition, even from New York taxi drivers.

His principal feature is that while he is not nosy – he won't ask you who you are or what you are or where you're from, unless you volunteer the information first – but he will tell you every goddam thing that is wrong with him from his swollen feet up to his headache.

I don't want to, as Cyril Connolly would say, 'make a thing about it', but the set-up regarding hospitals in America does not seem to compare very favourably with England, or even with Ireland. There must be something very wrong with a system which demands two hundred and fifty dollars (about eighty-five pounds) in advance, before a hospital will take you in.

PARK AVENUE

Which is exactly what happened to me. However, the truth is bitter, and I pay my American friends the compliment of telling them what I think.

I am told that not everyone all the time is happy, even in New York. There are broken hearts on the Great White Way. That's for sure. There are broken hearts everywhere, but not everyone has a broken heart at one and the same time.

On the average, a man in good health should not have his heart broken more than six times a year. Even the youngest and prettiest girl at Vassar College, my *Tir na n-Og* (my dream place, land of eternal youth) cannot get her heart broken more than nine times a year.

Heartbreak is only trouble. An unhappy love affair, the death of a parent or a child, these are only troubles. If you are in reasonably good health, have a room and adequate food, tobacco and the price of a drink, death and love can be mourned in comfort.

One's own ill health and death are unspeakable calamities and that is all I can say about them.

I am not a priest but a sinner. I am not a psychiatrist but a neurotic. My neuroses are the nails and saucepans by which I get my living. If I were cured, I would have to go back to house-painting.

They say in Irish, *Is fearr an timreas ná an tuaigneas* (quarrelling is better than loneliness) and to be poor is to be lonely. The prospect for a lonely poor person on Broadway is that he can walk around and look at the lights and there are more people to be touched for a dime.

I write of these things because one can find everything in New York, even the gravestone of the man who founded the Saint Patrick's Day parades. He was a Protestant schoolteacher from County Antrim in Ireland, and there was a purpose behind these parades originally, because they were instigated as a piece of defiance against the Ku Klux Klan and other kinds of nutty people of that sort who didn't like the Irish very much at the time. The Irish got together and paraded in the streets to show how many there were of them.

In Ireland of course, Saint Patrick's Day is observed as a religious festival, and up until about two years ago, the only place in Dublin where you could get a drink was at the Royal Dublin Society's Dog Show, which is held on that day. I was up there once with two painters, Séan O'Sullivan and Harry Kernoff, for to get a couple of drinks, and we paid our entrance money and mixed around with the Anglo-Irish and the imitation Irish and they'd put years on you with their awful tweedy hats. I think they make their hats from used kilts or something.

Naturally the dogs were barking and making noises as dogs will when they are confined to one place – the Lord Jesus, do not mention greyhounds, I have already had one lawsuit on my hands – when suddenly Séan O'Sullivan turned to Harry Kernoff and myself and said in amazement: 'Hell, what a place to bring dogs!' He had forgotten that it was a dog show.

Both Catholics and Protestants observe Saint Patrick's Day as a day of worship and to a certain extent the Jews celebrate it too, but they celebrate it quietly at home with a feed and some of that rabbinical wine which would kill a horse. They celebrate it as an Irishman but naturally not in the same way as a Christian. As a matter of fact, the Dublin or the Belfast Jew does not usually wear a shamrock, not for any insult to the shamrock, but for the simple reason that it represents the Blessed Trinity, the Father, Son and Holy Ghost, which is obviously not part of his faith.

Saint Patrick's Day in New York is the most fantastic affair, and in past years on Fifth Avenue, from Forty-fourth Street to Ninety-sixth Street, the white traffic lines were repainted green for the occasion. All the would-be Irish, has-been Irish and never-been Irish, seem to appear true-blue Irish overnight. Everyone is in on the act, but it is a very jolly occasion and I have never experienced anything like it anywhere else in the world.

I was asked to do a turn by a friend of mine, Max Gordon, at his night club, called the 'Blue Angel', which I agreed to do and a party of us went along, including a Jewish fellow whom I felt privileged to know and who I hope feels the same way about me. The doorman at the club happened to be Irish and because it was Saint Patrick's night, I asked him if there were many of our own in the place.

My Jewish friend turned to me:

'I hate that expression, "our own", Brendan,' he said. 'Everyone is your own,' which at the time I thought was very sound sense and furthermore I still do.

But he then explained to me that his father had come over to America to escape from the pogroms in tsarist Russia at the turn of the century and he went to work for one of his so-called 'own' – his uncle.

Now his uncle had him sorting rags for about fifteen cents an hour which even in 1900 wasn't an awful lot of money, but as the poor man was in a strange country and didn't understand any language except Russian and Yiddish, there was nothing much he could do about it.

'Well, there it was,' said my friend. 'There's your own for you.'

We went into the 'Blue Angel' and although I am not a professional in the gagging game, one section of my family have been in the theatre business and in show business generally, supplying costumes, running theatres, owning cinemas and all to that effect, for generations.

Anyway I got up and did my piece and I succeeded in making Shelley Berman laugh, and as he is a professional in the business, I consider him a fair critic. I can put on a show for an hour perhaps once in every two weeks, but I couldn't do as well as these professional guys every night. However, that night Berman laughed, and I don't think he was just being polite. Well, maybe he was. Afterwards we all sang Irish songs, some of which I made up myself.

There was a time when an Irishman, Dion Boucicault, was the most prolific author on Broadway. Nowadays, however, I think Broadway could stand three hundred and sixty-five Saint Patrick's days in the year, but if they had any more than two Yom Kippurs, an awful lot of places would be out of business.

I was invited by Leonard Lyons, the famous columnist on the New York *Post*, and by his wife, Sylvia, to attend the ceremony when Douglas, their son, was being Bar Mitzvahed, which is the Jewish confirmation.

Now in Ireland, a Catholic is not supposed to attend even the funeral of a Protestant friend, but when my wife asked a Jesuit friend of ours from a foreign university, Father Herbert Rogers, if we could go along, he replied at once that it was perfectly in order and he added: 'Make sure you bring Brendan with you. A visit to a house of divine worship is not going to do him any harm anyway.'

Synagogue on Rivington Street
(on Yom Kippur)

I presume perhaps the majority of my readers are not Catholics and they probably look upon the Jesuits as if they are witch doctors or something. Actually they are a body of highly intelligent men.

A few days before, I had had to go to Philadelphia to speak at Bryn Mawr College where there are very many lovely girls. I also spoke at Vassar College one time, where there are also many very lovely girls. They are young and fresh and educated and read books and talk about them. Their manners are so good that I was surprised that so much expense could produce so much cultivation; so much innocence and sophistication and so much elegance and youth. However, I am transgressing, or rather, digressing.

On the day of the Bar Mitzvah, we flew back from Philadelphia, and we arrived at the synagogue carrying our suitcases. We asked the girl in the cloakroom if we could leave them there until the Bar Mitzvah was over, and judging by the look on her face, I think she was saying to herself: what do these Micks think? Do they think this is a hotel? Are they going to ask me for a room or something?

So I reassured her.

'Look,' I said. 'We've just come from Philadelphia to attend the ceremony and we're very honoured by the invitation. We like Douglas and we like his parents. We are staying at the Algonquin Hotel which might be a consolation to you because, although we understand that a synagogue is a very hospitable institution and there's usually a banqueting hall attached to it, we certainly don't expect to be spending the night here – not in a bed at least.'

Her face assumed an expression of relief, if it ever can be so described, and we handed her the suitcases and she offered to take my coat.

About this coat. Hereby hangs another tale.

I bought it in Brooks Brothers and the chap who sold it to me must have recognized a right eejit, for he told me he was a landsman of mine, which is an American expression meaning that his ancestors came from Ireland, and he knew just the sort of coat I would like.

Now I don't know a lot about coats, but it was cashmere and certainly very warm.

'How much is it?' I asked.

59th STREET BRIDGE, 2nd AVENUE

'Two hundred and eighty dollars,' he replied.

The American may think that our pounds and ten shillings and florins and shillings and sixpences and threepenny-bits and pennies and ha'pennies are a bit extraordinary, but I cannot count money in any language. It doesn't mean anything to me. Although I had a show on Broadway at the time, I swear to God I didn't intend to pay one hundred pounds for an overcoat. I have known the day when I bought an overcoat for fifty shillings quite happily.

However I just handed the man the dollars and that was that.

Back in the Algonquin, a friend came over to admire the new purchase and asked me how much I had paid for it, so I told him.

'Brendan,' he said, 'do you know how much that is in your country?'

'No,' I said, 'I never thought about it.'

He called over an English waiter by the name of Bob Bennett.

'Tell me, Bob, how much is two hundred and eighty bucks in English money?'

'It's exactly one hundred pounds.'

'Oh,' I said, 'so I have paid one hundred pounds for an overcoat. Well, I can hardly go back now and ask them for something a little bit more reasonable. I shall just have to impress everyone with it back home in Ireland.'

'Listen, Brendan,' my friend said. 'You know if you'd paid another ten dollars for it, you could have impressed everyone in America by saying that you'd paid more for an overcoat than the President of the United States.'

However pride comes before a fall. I lost the overcoat – I couldn't have an hour's luck flaunting my glory before the world.

On the day of the Bar Mitzvah, however, I still had my two hundred and eighty dollar coat and I reluctantly handed it over.

At the service I was beside Frank Loesser, whom I don't think is any more madly religious than I am myself, and there was Ethel Merman, the singer, Paddy Chayefsky, the author of *Marty* and *The Tenth Man*, and numerous other notabilities, so I felt quite at home.

The altar boy, if that's the phrase, was wearing a silk shawl round his shoulders and looked extremely composed; but the Rabbi, with all due respect to the reverend gentleman, I think was a little over-

1st AVENUE, 10 & Street (SLAVIC DISTRICT)

come by his audience, and if my Jewish readers will pardon my saying so, well, he went on a bit.

Douglas, who was named for a justice of the American Supreme Court called William O. Douglas, who was also attending the ceremony, read beautifully from the Scriptures and I found it a marvellous affair.

After the service we went to the banqueting hall where we had a highly imaginative, sustaining, beautiful meal of meat wrapped up in cabbage leaves, gefüllte fish and beef, which oddly enough was cooked rather in the same way that the Catholic Irish used to cook it at home when I was a kid, and there was no damper on the champagne. Whether it was kosher champagne or not, I don't know, but it certainly tasted all right. So much so, that when all the guests began to dance the hora, we joined in, though neither my wife nor myself knew the dance, but we did know how to do the sixteen-handed reel, which is much the same thing.

Afterwards, I was introduced to William Douglas.

'I believe you're a judge of the American Supreme Court?' I said.

'Yes, that's right, Brendan,' he answered, 'but how did you know?'

'Well,' I said, 'I know you've got very good clothes and obviously you didn't come by them honestly, but on the other hand I knew you weren't a politician, because you look a little bit too honest.'

So he laughed and we all had a great time.

I must tell a story about the American Supreme Court and I refuse to reveal the source of the information because I do not want to get anybody into trouble.

It appears that Doctor Kinsey was invited to Washington to give a lecture on his famous work, *Sexual Behaviour in the Human Male*. After the lecture, one Supreme Court justice turned round to a colleague of his, also a Supreme Court justice, who was leaving the room, and said to him:

'I say,' he said. 'Did you hear what that fellow Kinsey said about all American youths masturbating during adolescence?'

'Well,' said the other justice, 'and what is wrong with that?'

'I certainly never did,' said the first.

So the other one replied: 'Well, you missed a damn good thing!'

This reminds me of a story I heard of a little boy who had been sent to Eton or Harrow or one of those posh public schools in England where they say the three principal factors in their education are: beating, bullying and buggery. The headmaster was interviewing the boy's mother and he asked her the little fellow's name.

'Master Bates,' came the reply.

'Oh, he does, does he,' said the headmaster. 'We'll soon cure him of that.'

The most beautiful clubs I have ever seen are in New York, except perhaps for the Roaring Twenties Club which is in Hollywood, and that was pretty fine. They had a fireman's pole down which the girls used to slide in the cabaret; but I believe all the girls came from New York so it entitles them to a place in this epic of mine.

Leonard Lyons, who is a very fit man and probably the fittest grandfather in the world, used to take me – and does yet if I go to New York – to every night club in the place but only if I am completely sober on the soda water, or the tea when I am able to get it. I don't like American coffee, English coffee or Irish coffee, though

Irish coffee is not bad if it has got a fair base of whiskey in it, or what the Irish call the 'stick' in it. Outside of Ireland it is usually referred to as Gaelic coffee, in the same way as our twenty-six counties are called Eire and our language, Gaelic. The only time that the Irish themselves use the word Gaelic in connection with our language, is if we happen to be speaking Gaelic, otherwise we call it Irish. If we are referring to Gaelic coffee, well in the more snobbish hotels in Dublin, Belfast or Cork, some of the Irish that would be there might call it Gaelic coffee, but on the whole we call it coffee with the 'stick' in it.

I think it is impertinence to call our country Eire. It is Ireland. If you are referring to Germany, you certainly would not say that you made a trip to Deutschland recently and drank Deutsch wine. For the matter of that, nor would you say that James Joyce lived in Zurich in Helvetia. (That is a bit of chauvinist propaganda that I should not really be bothered with, except that I might be preaching to the unconverted.)

However, Leonard Lyons used to take me on the rounds and we would usually start around midnight at Vincent Sardi's restaurant or perhaps Jim Downey's Steak House on Eighth Avenue, and off we would go to all the clubs.

The loveliest place I saw was the 'Four Seasons' which has a *Brasserie* which is open twenty-four hours a day, every day. It is an incredible restaurant and the decorations in the place change with the seasons, as well as the uniform of the waiters. The manager showed me a tapestry by Picasso which is a lovely thing, not that it requires any commendation from me, and he said:

'Now, doesn't that show you that we are a broadminded people? After all, Picasso is a Communist.'

'No,' I said, 'It simply shows that you would not be able to do the bloody tapestry as well as Picasso!'

In New York I saw some of the most beautiful art collections that I have ever seen in my life. I was in Governor Harriman's house and he has a splendid collection of paintings. He is a big, gentle, very kindly and highly intelligent man and his wife is an absolute encyclopedia on French art and knows a great deal more about it than several Parisians and Parisiennes whom I know. We were wandering about the house and my wife, who is also a painter, was charmed

with herself, and even I, a house-painter and kind of conditioned against art for some reason, was charmed. The only house-painter that I know who became a great art painter was Georges Braque – the Lord have mercy on him, he died last year – and he was also a considerable boxer and cyclist.

One of the guests in the Harriman's house on this occasion was not so well informed on art as perhaps she might have been. Now I don't say that everybody should be well informed on art, but on the other hand, I am not like W. B. Yeats, the Irish poet, who said that the theatre should be a secret society. Damn it, if the theatre was a secret society, I would still be whitewashing ceilings and climbing sixty-foot ladders, which would not be good for me at all.

This lady, however, was obviously from the top drawer of American society and I felt she should have known better. I am not setting myself up as a connoisseur of genuine aristocracy, but I am a terrific snob and on my mother's side, I am descended from a sixth-century king called Conal Cearnach, and I was privileged to receive an invitation to the inauguration of President Kennedy, whose brutal

CENTRAL PARK

assassination shocked every decent living man and woman throughout the world.

I was admiring one of the paintings and I said to my wife: 'It looks as if our hosts have also a " Douanier".'

So the lady, who was standing within earshot, and who I think felt she had to educate the 'Micks', turned to me and said:

'Actually, that painting is not by the person you mentioned. It's by a man called Henry Rousseau.'

'You mean,' I replied, 'Henri Rousseau,' pronouncing his name in my best French accent.

'Oh,' she said, 'is that what they call him?'

'Yes,' I said, 'but he is usually known as "Le Douanier" which is the French for a customs' officer, because that was his profession before he retired to devote his whole time to painting in Paris.'

One of the servants, or in the lovely civilized American phrase, 'one of the help', turned to me and whispered in my ear:

'Listen, Brendan, I bet that old bitch is going to throw herself down the elevator shaft now!'

The other story parallel to this, concerns a very famous American millionairess who was supposed to be something of an art fancier, though to tell the truth, I found her a bit of a phoney. There were two or three of us drinking in a bar and she came across to our table and asked if she might join us.

'What do you do?' she asked one fellow.

'I'm a sculptor.'

'And what do you do?' she asked the next man.

'I'm a painter.'

She turned to me. 'What about you?'

'Oh, I'm another painter,' I said and I didn't tell her I was only a house-painter, nor did I tell her I was trying to write, because I did not want any old lip from her. I did not like her and I did not notice any tendency on her part, for all her millions, to do the necessary and shout at the top of her voice: 'Garçon, treat my friends!'

Finally, she spoke to an American who was with us and asked him what he did, that was exciting.

'Madam,' he said. 'I mix Pernod with brandy!'

One of the most beautiful paintings I ever saw, which is in the Museum of Modern Art, is the original vast *Guernica*, by Pablo Picasso, which has to be seen to be believed, for it serves as a great warning against terrorism, violence and war. I had seen reproductions of it, but the reproductions do not give any idea of its extraordinary quality.

The only American artist I ever knew was the late Franz Kline, and I knew him quite well. He is up in heaven now, or wherever good artists go when they die.

I did meet, however, a great many American actors, and in some cases this made me very popular with other people who wanted to meet them, but in one case when I was staying for a few days in Boston it proved very unfortunate.

There was a very famous actor, an old but pleasant fellow who had very good manners indeed, but so far as was known, he was not interested very much in girls.

I was in the house of some Irish friends of mine where there was a very pretty girl of about eighteen summers, and she had heard that this actor was in Boston and said she would like to meet him. I said I thought this would be all right and the next time I saw this old fellow, I told him that I knew a little girl who was very anxious to make his acquaintance.

'O.K.' he said, 'I will see what night I can take her out or what night she is free to come out.'

Finally they made a date, and the girl's father, who was so Irish that he might never have left his native land, asked me if I thought his little girl would be quite safe going out with this Hollywood old-timer.

'My good man,' I replied, 'she couldn't possibly be safer,' and I did not explain the reason why I could make this statement with such assurance, because, first of all I don't think he would have understood what I meant, and secondly, if he had done, he would have thought I was mad.

So the girl met this old boy, and greatly to my surprise, he proceeded to date her all the time he was in Boston. After a while, he went away to Alaska to make a film, and I am quite certain he was not running away from the girl because he gave her the address, but she lost the damned thing.

Two or three months afterwards she explained to me that she was in a bit of trouble.

At the time, my money was being held for me – or held from me – and I was only allowed enough to go round the bare essentials, and certainly not the kind of money that was needed to help her out of trouble.

But the Lord is wondrous kind, for lo and behold, didn't a linen goods' company arrange with a well-known magazine for a competition that was the answer to this maiden's prayer, and I was to be one of the judges.

In the competition you had to write a letter saying why you would like to visit the Emerald Isle. (I discovered in England and in America that the Emerald Isle meant Ireland, though I never heard anyone else calling it this.)

The first prize was a sea trip to Ireland and a tour of the country with all expenses paid. Now much as I love my native land, it is not the sort of place where you would send a girl to have her little affairs sorted out.

Christmas Circus at the Coliseum

The second prize was three thousand dollars, and in my own mind, daughter, said I, we're in business, and the third prize was a week's visit to some suburb in New York State, which was just about as good as Ireland for our purpose, which was no good at all. It was as good as a hole in the head.

The two other judges on the panel were what are called in England, 'big heads'. One was a young up and coming Washington politician and the other a society hostess, famous for her *élite* parties and for bringing the rich together.

I went to the society-organizing lady and explained the position quite truthfully to her as she was a good old skin, and so far as I know, not in the least interested in men. At this stage of the game, I was so completely confused, however, that if somebody had told me that the head of the Methodist Church kept a harem, I would not have been at all surprised.

Anyway she was very understanding and said she would abide entirely by my decision.

Then I went to the politician and buttered him up with all sorts of nonsensical tales of how busy he was, when in actual fact he didn't have a damn thing to do, so far as I could see, except to be a kind of

Belly-dancers at the Egyptian Gardens, 8th Avenue

official 'greeter' to foreign potentates. Washington seems to supply a 'greeter' of every nationality under the sun. I shouldn't be surprised if they had someone to greet people from Andorra or Tibet.

'That's right, Brendan,' he said. 'After all, you're a writer so you should know. We'll let you judge the competition yourself.'

I am sure I am open to prosecution on this, but then Our Lord had mercy on Mary Magdalen and I can always plead the fifth commandment.

I told the girl how I had fixed everything up for her and even suggested writing the letter myself, though I don't like working for nothing. I mean, she was going to get the three thousand bucks.

'Oh no,' she said. 'I'm quite capable of writing the essay myself. I've been listening all my life to my family and my neighbours talking about Ireland and I feel I almost know as much about the country as you do.'

'I'll tell you one thing and that's not two, that you may not know,' I said, 'and that is that Ireland is the very last place on God's earth for you to go to have your troubles attended to, so I am going to see that you only get the second prize.'

After a while, the letters came in, and Jesus, Mary and Joseph, there must have been at least fifty thousand of them. My apartment was stacked with letters from all sorts of people, not only Irish, but from every nationality, who all seemed to be after, either a trip to Ireland or the three thousand dollars. I don't think many of them would have been too anxious to spend a week in a New York State suburb. However, there is no accounting for taste.

Not knowing the girl's handwriting, I had to search and search and search through the mountainous pile until I eventually found her letter. I marked it in red pencil, 'This is the second prize'. At random I picked two other letters, one from somebody with a Jewish name and the other from a Frenchman. I mean, I was giving everyone a fair shake. Actually, the Frenchman had written the better essay of the two, so I marked his letter the first prize. Then I went to the linen company.

'Listen,' I said, 'here are the three letters that we have chosen as winners of your very excellent competition.' I would have said 'after much thought' but I didn't like to push my luck.

Unfortunately for me, the public relations officer of the linen importers, chose to read the letters for himself and decided that my girl's letter was deserving of the first prize.

'Oh no,' I complained. 'Good God, her grammar does not entitle her to the first prize.'

Now I know as much about grammar as my backside does about snipe shooting, which is not very much, but it was a desperate situation and I had to knock the girl to help her. Finally I prevailed upon the man to change his mind.

'Do you want to reduce her letter to the third prize?' he asked.

'Ah no,' says I, 'she deserves second prize. Grammar isn't everything.'

Now the girl lived in an Irish section of Boston where I am afraid the quality of mercy is strained with regard to matters of this sort, but they are very good people and they may be right. I am speaking very seriously for, after all, we were committing a mortal sin, but the just man falls seven times and it wasn't my fault. We had to think of some good reason for the girl to leave this community for a while, so we told her father, a most fearsome gentleman I may say, that a branch of an Irish organization for girls was being formed way out in another State, a few hours' journey away, and that the girl was anxious to join them for a few weeks.

'Well now,' he said, 'I'm very pleased to see my daughter taking an interest in the old country. I never knew her to be interested in anything except Rock and Roll before.'

'Oh,' I said, 'at the back of it your daughter is very patriotic towards Ireland,' which was a complete lie. She liked Ireland but she was more interested in doing the Twist and in the old actor.

We went on a train up to the place and to see the doctor, who was not a quack and was acting more from humanitarian reasons than from any other, but he had to live. He put her in his clinic. When she gave him the three thousand dollars, he handed her back one thousand, which I thought was very civil of him.

I went up to collect her afterwards and on the way back in the train, we went into the club car to have a drink, for by God, I needed it. I started telling her the history of the revolutionary movement in Ireland, which bored her stiff I may say, but her sudden new-found interest in the land of her ancestors had to be explained some way.

I taught her rebel songs, some of which were written by an uncle of mine, who, the Lord have mercy on him, would not have been at all pleased at the transaction.

Finally, I brainwashed her about the cause of old Ireland and being only eighteen, she had a good memory, although she got a little bit mixed up occasionally. The worst thing was that some of the people in the club car were either Irish or they simply liked these kind of songs and they all joined in!

After I had delivered her safely home, I moved right back down midtown as quick as ever I could and I seriously considered going even further, to Kennedy airport.

YANKEE STADIUM

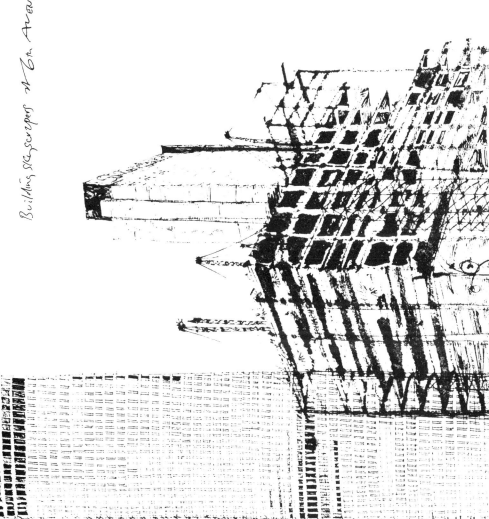

Building skyscrapers on 5th Avenue

Statue of Liberty

What are they at round Broadway and the bars?

In 1959, during the Theatre Festival in Paris, the Paris Theatre Society entertained the authors of the plays at the Theatre des Nations, at which, I am proud to say, my play *The Hostage* represented Great Britain, later to win the award for the best play of the year. I was not proud of it representing Great Britain but because it was being acted by perhaps the finest actress in the English language.

I was quite a big shot at this Festival and we were taken first to the Martini Building in the Champs-Elysées, there to be entertained with vermouth, which is a drink that I don't take unaccompanied. The Martini people were very understanding however, and they saw to it that I drank what the Americans call a Martini, which is certainly not entirely vermouth.

Afterwards the Paris Theatre Society brought us out by coach to Versailles, where I had been once before, just after the war, with two Americans and both New Yorkers. One of them, with typical New York restlessness, had left Dublin University where he was supposed to be studying on the G.I. Bill and the other one was at the Sorbonne.

In my very early days in Paris, I had met many New Yorkers, some of them now famous, such as Norman Mailer, who wrote *The Naked and the Dead*, and Jimmy Baldwin who has done so much to help

integration. It would be insulting to call him a Negro writer, just as I do not like to be called a working-class writer.

There was an old lady in our party at this Theatre Festival who said that she was as old as the Statue of Liberty, and that her parents had known Gustave Eiffel in the days when he designed the framework of the statue, eighty years ago. And people said at the time that neither the Eiffel Tower nor the Statue of Liberty would stand up, but by God, I am pleased to say that Paris still has the Eiffel Tower and New York Harbour still has this splendid, welcoming woman right there.

She was a gift to America from France and a monument to commemorate the alliance between the two nations during the American Revolution. And she was designed over-all by Frederic Auguste Bartholdi.

It drives me insane to realize the chance I missed because I did not climb up inside the lady to her head, even if only to say that I was inside the Statue of Liberty. But she is not entirely hollow because she has a heart, a heart for the poor, for the distressed, for the wealthy and for the successful.

MANHATTAN SKY-LINE

There is no more kindly welcome in the world than this Statue, as she stands in New York Harbour at the very gate of the New World. For eighty years, she has given hope and courage to millions of people.

At this point I would like to make it clear that I am not interested in politics – which are neither Fascism, Communism nor rheumatism – but the Statue of Liberty, Gustave Eiffel's second great symbol of a great city, has brought peace to many millions, from Syria to Connemara in the far west of Ireland. And peace, apparently, is not the only thing she brings, for on a board outside one public house in Connemara hangs the notice: 'You had better stop and have a drink here, because you won't find another saloon until you get to Brooklyn!'

The skyline of Manhattan is best seen off one of the ferries which go round the Island two or three times a day. It's a pleasure trip, and most certainly is a pleasure trip. I went round once with Captain Sheridan on his boat and when I am in New York, I intend to go round again. You may think that I want to go round with Captain Sheridan merely because he is obviously of Irish descent, but such is not the case. The man is a friend of mine and it is a trip that should not be missed. You can see the Island better than you can from an aeroplane, even.

I knew somebody in New York who had a friend on the Port Authority – everybody knows somebody in New York who knows somebody else – and he offered to take me up in a helicopter, and I had to plead that I had a hangover, which was a lie, because for a year in New York City I did not drink anything except soda water and tea. It was simply cowardice on my part.

I love skyscrapers and neon lights. They are so homelike, safe and reassuring. Manhattan is a mother clasp.

Piccadilly at midnight is dark and deserted. Unless you are a police-man, a criminal or a prostitute, you have no business there. In the centre of London after eleven p.m., if you are not at home listening to the night prayers on the BBC, you may be robbed, raped or arrested.

Broadway is not lonely at any hour of the day or night because it is a complete blaze of colour and you can get anything you want there twenty-four hours a day. It is a tribute to the twentieth century, and also to the late nineteenth century, when there were playhouses on Broadway, and oddly enough, fully fifty per cent of them were Irish plays. Not the Abbey Theatre kind, or stuff of that sort for the culture vulture who wants to hear an Irish dialect that never existed on land or sea, but good old melodrama where a British officer is trying an Irish rebel at a court martial, and he suddenly goes mad, jumps up and says: 'I may be an English officer, but I am also an Irish gentleman!'

Broadway never closes, though most of the theatres nowadays are off the main drag. The Metropole on Broadway goes in solely for entertainment and, I understand, is the birthplace of the Twist. Now I am afraid that the Twist came a little bit late for Brendan Francis Behan, but I would like to see a drawing of myself attempting to do it. My wife is a pretty good Twister. I do not intend any pun!

On Broadway itself there is a statue of George Michael Cohan who wrote most of the songs that the American Expeditionary Force sang in France during the First World War, including 'Over There' and 'Give My Regards to Broadway'. At this point I would like to give my regards to Broadway for to get Broadway to give its regards to me.

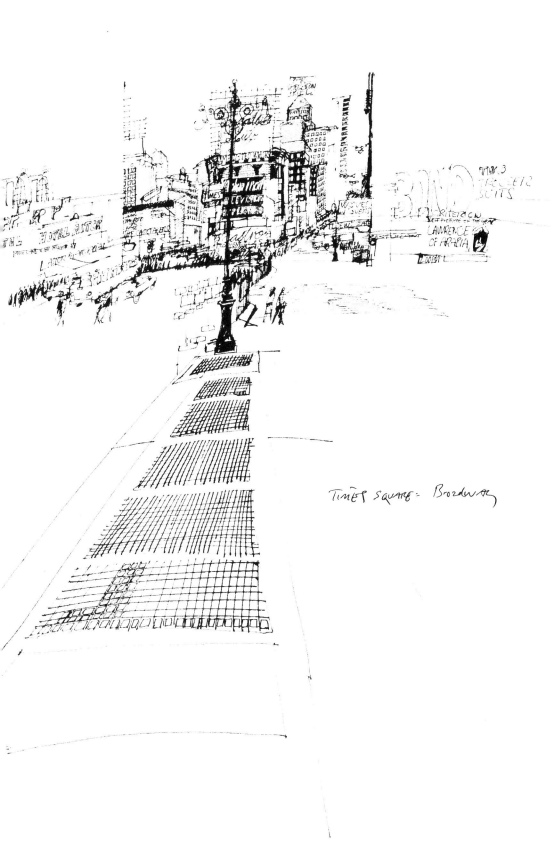

TIMES SQUARE = Broadway

Above: In the Grandstand at the Big "A" (the Aquaduct Race Track)

Opposite: Eddie Ginevan at the Big "A"

At the other end of Broadway, further down from Times Square, is another statue of a man who was also very intimately connected with the doughboys of the First World War, Father Duffy.

Saint Patrick's Cathedral was packed at his funeral and the police were standing round trying to keep the crowd in some kind of order. It was attended by mayors and governors and ordinary New York people from every denomination: Catholics, Protestants, Jews and I suppose other religions that I don't know about, because I know in New York they have a church to cater for everybody, just as they have a night club to cater for everybody.

It is said that an old New Yorker went up to one of the policemen. 'Listen,' he said, 'you've got to let me in.'

'I'm sorry,' the cop replied, 'but the place is full.'

'You've got to let me in, Officer,' the poor old New Yorker pleaded, 'I was a friend of Father Duffy's.'

'Look Mac,' came the reply, 'that is true of everybody in this city.'

There are many very famous restaurants on Broadway and I have chewed many excellent theatrical steaks at Jim Downey's Steak House which, like 'Vincent Sardi's', is packed with actors, some of

them doing very well, otherwise neither Mr. Sardi nor Mr. Downey would be able to use the kind of automobiles they do, while other actors, as the saying has it, are resting.

I went racing many times with Jim Downey at the Aqueduct Race Track, or the 'Big A.' as it is generally called. It is a beautiful course and the only way I can describe it is by calling it a luxury racecourse compared to anything we have in Ireland. It is all escalators and coffee bars and bars. I found the place betting at the window was the best way to win money, though you can only bet at the pari-mutuel windows in America for they do not go in for bookies.

I was given several winners however by Eddie Ginevan, a friend of Jim Downey's, whom we used to meet, either at the 'Big A.' or the Belmont Race Track, and he would introduce me to the various people in the racing business. As far as I know, his son trained horses or rode them and I think he trained some for Jim.

A Broadway author – I am proud to call myself one – always waits, on the first night of his play, either in 'Sardi's' or 'Downey's', and his press agent goes out to get the six newspapers, which are called 'the Six Butchers of Broadway'.

Now if you get six out of six good reviews, you could ask the President of the United States to sell you the White House, though I don't think this has ever happened. If you get five good reviews, you are doing fairly well and you have to start worrying about 480, Lexington Avenue, which is the home of the income tax. It is not a bad kind of worry though in its own way, if you have got to have worries, and I suppose everyone has to have them. If you have four, you can afford to give a party, or at least you can afford to attend the party which is usually given for you.

If you get three good reviews, it's time like to go home to bed, but if you only get two, you stay there the whole of the following day and don't go out until after dark. If you get one good review, you just make an air reservation very quickly to get back to where you came from, but if you get six bad reviews, you take a sleeping pill. You might even take an overdose!

However, I think I got five or six good reviews. Enough to keep me in business anyway. I know Walter Kerr of the New York *Herald-Tribune* and Howard Taubman of *The New York Times* were both enthusiastic over *The Hostage* and they are the really important reviewers. No, I forget. They are all important. I will be writing another play!

Actually, I got pretty good reviews and when I went into 'Sardi's' that night, the crowd stood up and clapped. It is said that there is jealousy amongst authors in New York, but I didn't see it. Perhaps it exists, but I didn't find it.

Jack Dempsey, the heavyweight boxer, also has a restaurant on Broadway and he is a very kindly fellow and he invited me to lunch one time. During the course of the very excellent meal, he told me that somebody asked him, after he had retired, what he was going to do with all his money.

'I'm opening a restaurant on Broadway,' he replied.

'Gene Tunney,' they said, 'he is using his money to go to Harvard to study Shakespeare.'

'Well,' said Jack Dempsey, 'if it helps Gene's racket, it's O.K. by me.'

Gene Tunney was a tremendous man and a great New Yorker. When I told him this story, he corrected me and said that he wasn't

Peep Show on 42nd Street

going to Harvard to study Shakespeare, but he was going to Yale to lecture on Shakespeare. I have a photograph of himself with Colonel Eddie Egan of the New York Boxing Commission and Bernard Shaw, who had a tremendous interest in the manly art and whose novel, *Cashel Byron's Profession*, was all about boxing when it was illegal in England. Cashel Byron, like Gene Tunney, was an intellectual heavyweight.

As far as I remember, Gene Tunney told me that his mother went to his fights, but his father never did because he wasn't interested very much in boxing.

I was lunching one time with Gene Tunney in the Saints and Sinners Club, at which there were a great many journalists and policemen. Now I am a friend of all the New York reporters – I wouldn't say all the Hollywood reporters, because although most of them are all right, there are a few, I think, that the nation could do without – but I could hardly describe myself as a friend of all the policemen.

Reporters everywhere are attacked on many grounds, but in journalism, on the whole, the public get what they want. Well, I am sure a lot of people get fed up with *Pravda*, but then I am quite sure

In the Times Square Subway

that a lot of reporters get fed up with writing it. Perhaps this applies to the New York papers as well, though the only thing I object to about them, is their weight. It nearly requires a truck to take them home if you're wanting to read them all.

Now the connection between journalists and cops outside working hours in New York is a peculiar one

Each year, the New York Reporters Association, with the typical great-heartedness that they have – I don't speak for their employers because I am a newspaper man myself – run a ball for the Damon Runyon Cancer Fund and this is organized, about half and half, by the New York reporters and by the police department.

Because they all knew me, I got an invitation, and, if I say so myself, I was given the biggest clap of the evening after I had sung a few songs, even though I had competition from such genuine artists as Elizabeth Seal. I don't say this from vanity, or because I deserved it. The circumstances are this.

Some of the show was extremely up to date and, shall I say, the ladies were in a very advanced state. I mean they did not encumber

themselves with fur coats, and the police and the reporters started to clap these dancing and singing acts from the girls, until their wives looked round very disapprovingly and they had to stop.

When I got up and sang a sentimental Irish song that I had written myself, all the wives thought I was a wholesome Irish boy and they gave me the biggest clap of the evening.

The National Broadcasting Company and the Columbia Broadcasting System are not very far from Broadway and I have appeared on both, and they are an excellent body of people and extremely hospitable. I speak from experience because most of the broadcasting people I know, simply push you out the tradesmen's entrance after the show.

I was on the Jack Paar Show many times and was interviewed by Arlene Francis, and the only thing I objected to was the food. I am inclined to judge television organizations by what they give to eat and drink and, for some reason, these fantastically wealthy people supply food in cartons, which I don't eat anyway. Well, I suppose if I did not have any choice, I would have to. Perhaps they are afraid to

give any particular named brand of food, in case one of their adver-
tisers discovered that his rival's frozen steak was being patronized
and took his custom elsewhere.

The National Broadcasting Company, a subsidiary of RCA, is
located in a huge building called the RCA building, in Rockefeller
Center. But on one corner – separate from it – there is a saloon called
Hurley Brothers and Daly. The Hurleys and Mr. Daly were offered
some fantastic sum of money – as much money as there is in Fort
Knox – for to sell their restaurant, but they refused to do so. They
never look at television themselves – for which they have my full
blessing – and they haven't even television in the saloon.

A great number of people do not seem to realize that much of New
York, especially down past the Wall Street financial area, is very old
and it is not difficult to get there on a Broadway bus. I don't recom-
mend it however, for the public transport is so bad that our beautiful
Dublin City green double-decker buses would be a sensation on
Fifth Avenue. Also I have never, anywhere, except in New York and
Ibiza, seen an unfortunate man trying to double the jobs of driver
and conductor as he has to on the buses in these two places.

However, the busy financial area, on a late Saturday afternoon or
a Sunday, is peaceful enough and the narrow, usually crowded streets,
are empty and the tall buildings are all the more impressive for that.

They tell me that the Stock Exchange is a marvellous place, though
I was never in it, but I did go to see two beautiful churches nearby,
Trinity Church and St. Paul's Chapel which is on Broadway between
Vesey and Fulton Street.

St. Paul's Chapel is one of the finest examples of eighteenth-
century architecture in New York and is well worth a visit because
it caters for all sections of political opinion. Admiral Lord Howe is
remembered, who was Commander-in-Chief of the British Forces
in 1776 during the American War of Independence and there is also
the pew where George Washington worshipped. In the New York
Public Library there is an etching by Joseph Wright from a drawing
he made of Washington while he was actually attending service in
the church, and it is supposed to be one of the few authentic
portraits of him.

The St. Paul's altarpiece was designed by a Frenchman, the chan-

Broadway

The Emmet Memorial, ST PAUL's churchyard, Broadway
between VESEY and FULTON street

deliers are Waterford Irish glass and the chancel chairs, William and Mary period. In the churchyard, there is a granite obelisk memorial to Thomas Addis Emmet who was the brother of the famous Irish patriot Robert Emmet, and a great Irish patriot himself. He died in New York and was buried there, but later his body was removed to the family vault in Dublin.

The monument was put up through the efforts of William Mac-Neven – to whose memory also stands a granite shaft in the corner of the churchyard for saving New York from the cholera – although MacNeven and Emmet were of different faiths; Emmet was a member of the Church of Ireland and MacNeven a Catholic. And the inscriptions on it are in English, Irish and Latin, although oddly enough, the one in Irish was composed by a man called England. He was a Catholic Bishop.

The Irish societies in New York who are so fond of running round the place and doing all sorts of things on Saint Patrick's Day that are certainly not done in either Dublin, Belfast, Cork or Limerick, and wearing imitation shamrocks, they might do well to have the inscriptions renewed on the obelisk which have faded from age, although they are still almost legible, or at least if they got me a sculptor, I would pay for the inscriptions to be renewed myself.

I don't think much is left of the Washington Market, although I heard some fantastic tales of people buying bear steaks there once, and lion chops and tiger spareribs and meats of that sort. Near St. Paul's Chapel is the Fulton Fish Market which is very much in existence. The noise there, early in the morning, is absolutely deafening, and unless you wanted a free swim, and there are more comfortable ways of doing this in New York, it would be better to wait until later on in the day when the roar has stopped and the ice isn't spilling and melting all round. However, I've no doubt you could buy suitable clothing on the spot, for as I say, New York caters for everything.

There are stalls and stalls and stalls of every fish imaginable, and although most of them are now brought in by truck, there are still a few fishing vessels out at the very end of the pier. Anyone who has ever tasted fish that has come straight out of the sea, would never want to have it any other way. Maybe a glass of stout would improve it even more, though not American beer. I was never able for it and drank foreign beer most of the time.

The oldest saloon in New York is McSorley's Old Ale House which is quite famous and where the hard stuff is not sold at all. Amongst other relics that the owner has, is a Fifty Dollar Bond issued by the Irish in America in 1865 for raising money for revolutionary purposes. The Irish taught a great number of people, including the Jews, how to raise money in America, and the Israelis issued their own bonds in 1948.

On the bond is written that the fifty dollars are redeemable on the establishment of a native government in Ireland. My own political prejudices do not allow me to say that Ireland is entirely free yet. However, the bond is redeemable in Ireland because the first government we had there shortly after the signing of the Anglo-Irish Treaty in 1921, took them in and paid out the cash on them. Now I am very far from being a mathematician, but a bond issued in 1865 for fifty dollars, if presented at the Irish Consulate in New York to be sent home, would be worth something pretty considerable, for the Irish government would pay, not alone the fifty dollars, but the interest on it from 1865 as well.

I explained this to the boss in 'McSorley's', because New York is the only city in the world where I know the owner of a saloon has a valuable certificate worth a great deal of money and refuses to sell it.

'I know that,' he said, 'and I've never heard an F.B.I. man come in here, but he didn't tell me so.'

'I'm not in the F.B.I.,' I said. 'Not but what I had a swim with a guy from the F.B.I. and I actually succeeded in getting him to drink a glass of bourbon with me afterwards. But at the same time, I am not the sort of person who would be making very good police material. What the hell do you mean, F.B.I.? What have the F.B.I. got to do with it?'

'You are F.B.I.,' he repeated.

'Look,' I said, 'I had a swim with a guy that I met, that's all. I think you must be mad and furthermore, the F.B.I. will take a libel action against you.'

'You don't know what F.B.I. means, do you?' he said. 'What do you call us?'

'You're an Irish-American.'

'Yeh, I know, but amongst yourselves, what do you call us?'

'Narrowbacks,' I said.

'Well,' he said, 'do you know what we call you, amongst ourselves?'

I shook the head.

'F.B.I. Foreign-born Irish.'

McSorley's has been there for about a hundred years and is worth a visit from anybody of any sort, size, shape or creed, apart from being Irish, just to meet the old New Yorkers and hear them describe the place as Sloan painted it. Not that it has changed a deal. They sit round an oven and tell the most marvellous stories about Jimmy Walker, the Lord have mercy on him, and Al Smith, who had formerly worked at the Fulton Fish Market. Now I don't think anybody, even in the United States, will describe Al Smith as being left wing, yet the first thing he did, when he became Governor of New York State, was to release Jim Larkin, the Irish Socialist leader, from

FULTON STREET Fishmarket

Sing Sing. Larkin had been jailed in 1917 for what is called 'criminal syndicalism'.

But the conversation in the saloon is great on New York, which of course these old men do not appreciate now, for they remember the time when the buildings were half the size. They certainly do not appreciate the Time-Life building, nor for the matter of that, the Empire State Building.

The first McSorley was quite a sensible, but rather puritanical man. Strange as this may sound coming from one of the foreign-born Irish, unfortunately America, amongst other things, is a rather puritanical country.

But the original McSorley would not sell hard liquor and he would not allow a woman in the place, and to this day you will get an excellent pint of ale and an onion sandwich, but you will get no malt and no mots.

If you are interested in seeing a wonderful saloon which has not changed in a century, and in an almost hundred-year-old bond, and in good ale and raw onions, and in the fact that you can leave your wife outside with an excellent excuse, because she is not allowed in, then this is the place. Well, I don't suggest that you go there on a day when it is raining or snowing, except perhaps she could go to another saloon or she could go next door and have a cup of tea or coffee. The proprietor wouldn't even allow my wife inside and she had to stand outside while I brought her out a mug of ale.

Another saloon, which was practically my second home in New York, is 'Costello's' on Third Avenue, where there is a small but concentrated Irish section. It was owned by two brothers from the County Offaly in Ireland, Tim and Joe Costello, alas, both of whom are now dead.

Tim had been in the Irish Republican Army at home and he'd also been a taxi driver in Dublin, on St. Stephen's Green, with which I have many connections. My father and mother courted there, and they were also married at the University Church, which is a beautiful little Byzantine building designed by Cardinal Newman, or at least he suggested its design.

Tim was in Ireland at the beginning of the Free State Government and had subsequently got out and founded this saloon, which is also

McSorley's Old Ale House

life good it be
gone
INDIANS
PALE ALE
ONE YEAR OLD
20¢

a restaurant and where I have eaten many large steaks and will again with the help of God.

He would come over and sit at the table with me and he'd talk about old times in Ireland. The conversation would be mostly about the corruption, because everybody seems to take a pride in believing that their country is a little bit more corrupt than anybody else's.

But Tim was quite famous and many authors, artists and reporters used to get in there. I picked up the expression, 'get in there' from a bricklayer friend of mine, who went to work amongst the bright lights of Shrewsbury in England, which dear God, had I the chance of sweeping the streets of Broadway or being Lord Mayor of Shrewsbury, I think I would sweep the streets of Broadway. It would be more fun.

However, people eat, drink and make love in Shrewsbury, just as much as they do any place else, I suppose.

Thurber, before his eyesight went against him, did some of his most famous drawings on the walls in 'Costello's' and was a great friend of Tim's, who has subsequently had them incised so that they will be there permanently, or at least for as long as 'Costello's' will be there, which I hope is for a hundred years.

Hemingway left a stout shillelagh, snapped in two in a test of strength, which is still there and McNulty left his hat, now hanging above the bar. A frequent visitor was Walt Kelly, the cartoonist of 'Pogo' in the New York *Post*, as well as H. L. Mencken, the famous American journalist.

I most certainly would not wish to offend any cash customers of mine who might be members of the Rotary, but Mencken said that Rotary was pretty strong in Dublin, even amongst the very honest businessmen of my native city. He seemed to be a little bit more cynical than I am, for he told me that every time he heard members at a Rotary luncheon sob, he knew somebody was going to be screwed.

I met Alexander Woollcott too in 'Costello's' and he was a most charming person. But they all enjoyed Tim because he had a certain humour that you would only find in the midlands of Ireland. That is to say in the flat country, for it is a kind of flat humour, told with a flat accent.

JOHNNY GALLAGHER, COSTELLO'S

MA O'BRIEN'S, 3rd AVENUE & 94 Street

Mrs. Costello, Tim's widow, still owns the saloon and Johnnie Gallagher, the barman, is still there to the good. I send them my respects.

I tried to persuade Mrs. Costello to allow Paul Hogarth to make a drawing of her for this book, but she said: 'Ah, no. My day for having drawings made of my beauty is long since gone.'

Across the avenue from 'Costello's', there used to be 'Jimmy Glennon's', unhappily now defunct. I understand that Jimmy Glennon, during the war, was entertaining some naval personnel and discovered himself out in the Pacific instead of being behind his bar, the following morning.

Further up Third Avenue is 'Ma O'Brien's', where there was a great friend of mine, Tommy McCormick, who formerly owned a public house in Dublin. He told me that one of his regular customers one time in Dublin was a man who was inspecting some flats belonging to Guinness's brewery. They were working-class flats and this man was a very high-up official in the brewery, and he would drop in from time to time for to have a jar and a drop of the malt.

There was this day when, besides himself in the bar, there was an old lady sitting in the corner and a seaman who had just returned from a trip.

'There you are, God bless you, son,' said the old lady. 'Where did you go this time?'

'We went up to Egypt,' the seaman replied.

'Where is that?'

'Up around the corner of the North Pole.'

'Did you get sea-sick?'

'No,' the man said, 'I got a bit sick of going up, because you're going up a hill all the time. You know, the world is round.'

'That's right,' the old lady replied. 'I've seen the world on a globe.'

'Coming down was all right though, because we just freewheeled from the North Pole to Ireland and here I am. Now, how about a drink?'

'Oh, I wasn't thinking of any such a thing.'

'Come on. Take something.'

So the seaman got her a glass of whiskey, which is about four times the measure you'd get in any bar in America or England or Wales – an American or an Englishman could swim in it, let me tell you – and before he left, he bought her another one.

The old lady now turned her attentions to the high official at Guinness's brewery, whom she presumed would be both a Protestant and a gentleman.

'There you are, sir,' she said, talking in his direction. 'I got two beautiful glasses of whiskey off that young sailor boy, if I never had one glass of Guinness.' And she deliberately said Guinness, because no working-class person in Dublin ever asks for the drink by name, but simply asks for 'a glass' or 'a bottle', because they presume there isn't any other kind of beer except Guinness.

'Yes,' said the tall Guinness executive, 'so I'd noticed,' and he called over to Tommy McCormick for a small whiskey. Just as in the case of Guinness, Irish people, especially of the more respectable classes, never say a glass of Irish, because it is understood that blended Scotch is a drink for commercial travellers and not for gentlemen.

The old lady gave out the hint several more times.

'If I had a glass of Guinness now, it would cool the whiskey beautifully in my stomach,' she said.

'I've no doubt,' the man answered, tapping on the bar and ordering for himself another whiskey.

At six o'clock in the evening, the Angelus bell rang out and the woman proceeded to say her prayers. Presently, another old one came into the pub and the first old lady nodded like to inform her that she was saying the Angelus. When she finished, she crossed herself and as she was doing so, she called across: 'Maureen, what would you ever think of that old Orange bastard over there, that wouldn't buy me a glass of Guinness?'

'P. J. Clarke's' is also on Third Avenue, and in the saloon there is a photograph of myself with Kevin McGlory, an Irish-American film star, and a former Lord Mayor of Dublin, Robert Briscoe. I am sorry to say that Mr. Briscoe fell amongst thieves and he addressed some of the Irish societies who attacked me without reading a line of what I had written, or going to either of my plays.

However, Robert Briscoe was a very great Irishman and a brave soldier of the Irish Republican Army during 'The Troubles'. On several occasions he only missed death by inches at the hands of the British Secret Service, and I still think myself highly honoured to be in this photograph with him and the film star.

I was in 'P. J. Clarke's' one time when I met Franchot Tone, the actor, who was sitting with some friends of his. He shouted out to me: 'Hello, you old Irish bastard.'

Now, in a certain part of the world, these are fighting words, so I went over, and to say the least of it, I was very rude to him. Subsequently somebody explained to me that these were not fighting words at all. They were simply a good old American way of expressing affection amongst Catholics, Protestants or Jews whether they were Irish, English, Estonian or any other nationality.

Unfortunately an American columnist got hold of it and announced in his paper that Mr. Franchot Tone and myself had had a row.

Apart from the fact that I have the greatest respect for Franchot Tone as an actor – I remember him as a very young man in a film called *Susie* about the First World War, in which he appeared with the late and lovely Jean Harlow, and I've also seen him in many films since – I also know his family history and he is a collateral descendant

P J CLARKE'S, 3rd AVENUE

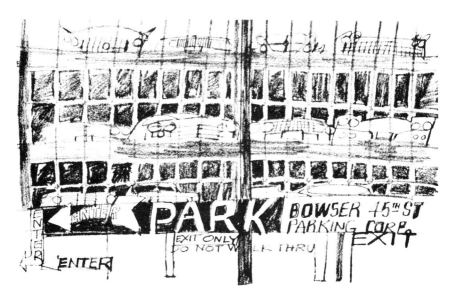

95th Street Car Park

of Theobald Wolfe Tone, the father of Irish Republicanism, who died in jail after the French invasion in 1798.

Later, I was able to apologize to him and explain that I wasn't acquainted with all the customs in America. I hope he reads this book, or if any of his friends do, they will remind him that I have the greatest respect for him, for his seed, breed and generation.

I was going up Third Avenue on one occasion and decided to stop off at Kearney's saloon to have a jar, when a man came up to me in the street. 'Hello,' he said.

'Hello,' I answered and went to walk away from him.

'You don't know who I am, do you?' he continued.

'Should I?' I asked, and I do not want to sound conceited, but strangers do come up to me in the street and welcome me like a long-lost cousin. This time it happened to be true, however.

'Do you mean to say,' the man said, 'that Kathleen Kearney's son is walking away from Patrick MacGuinness?'

Incidentally, the name MacGuinness, as I informed members of

the Guinness family who make the *vin noire* – the black wine of Ireland and a very good drink indeed – means the son of Angus, the God of Love. My grandmother was a Miss MacGuinness and so this chap was my mother's first cousin, and her favourite one, at that.

'Oh, hell,' I said. 'I didn't know you were Patrick MacGuinness, but how would I? Come on in to 'Kearney's' and we will have a drink.'

It turned out that he owned a farm somewhere north of the County Dublin, but he never went back there as he was fed up with the farming trick and rented it out. He had been in New York for many, many years.

The funny thing was that he wanted to talk all the time about Ireland, and as I had only left about three weeks before, I did not feel qualified to speak as a fully fledged exile. I hadn't yet acquired a romantic notion about my native land. I remember somebody, in the course of celebrating Saint Patrick's Day, remarking to me how much they loved the harp.

IRISH SALOONS on 8TH AVENUE

'Well,' I said, 'if you lived in Ireland and you saw a letter with a harp on it coming through the letter box, your heart would stop, because a harp usually means the Government, and that generally means, income tax.'

However, we eventually talked about the family and I promised to meet him again, which I did on sundry other occasions with his wife, and many a good evening we had.

MiKe SHEEHAN'S BAR, 3rd AVENUE. East 93rd street

WALL
STREET

STOCK EXCHANGE

JIM DOWNEY

PLACING BETS and VIEWING the RACE
ON closed-circuit television at the BIG "A"

FULTON STREET Fishmarket

Mc Sorley's old Ale House

MANHATTAN from Brooklyn

MANHATTAN Bridge from SOUTH street

HOTEL CHELSEA, 23 Street

Down-Town Up-Town and in and out of Harlem

The Hotel Chelsea is a marvellous institution and is lovingly called by a great many people, 'The Dowager of Twenty-third Street', because, as far as I know, it is the oldest building there, and is the heart and home of the street.

Built entirely of red brick, it is rather a splendid example of late-Victorian architecture, and every one of the ten floors has a beautiful little balcony of cast iron.

I had an apartment there which was extremely comfortable.

For nearly a hundred years many famous people have either lived or stayed there, and it was the hotel that the late Dylan Thomas occupied when he was in New York. And I am told by his wife, Caitlin, that it was the one where he was most happy. The Lord have mercy on him, for he died in St. Vincent's Hospital, a little way down the street.

Keidrych Rhys, a friend of Dylan Thomas and a Welsh speaker, as well as being the editor of the Welsh edition of the *People* – in England there is an edition of most newspapers to suit everyone, but if you want to get some information about the goings on in swimming pools at midnight bathing parties, then get the London edition – told me that Dylan pronounced his name Dullan, which is a fact that I don't think many people realize.

There is a plaque to his memory outside the Hotel Chelsea, on which there are also the names of Arthur B. Davies, James T. Farrell, Robert Flaherty, O. Henry, John Sloan, Thomas Wolfe and Edgar Lee Masters.

James Farrell wrote perhaps the finest account, next to James Joyce, of an Irish Catholic family, in *Studs Lonigan*, which is about a house-painter who becomes very fond of drink at the age of six. A fellow-feeling makes us wondrous kind. But Farrell was a very considerable writer as indeed was Wolfe, Flaherty and O. Henry.

To praise the wonderful work of Dylan Thomas would be an impertinence, but it is overshadowed by his adventures in the drinking line, if you can call drink an adventure, that is.

However, the Hotel Chelsea respects him as a great artist, and I would hope that Mr. Bard, the proprietor, and his son Stanley, who has a beautiful baby daughter, would leave space on their plaque for myself. I am not humble enough to say that I do not deserve one, but I hope it does not come too soon, because of all the names on the plaque, as far as I know, James T. Farrell is the only one that's alive and kicking very much.

I also met in the hotel Arthur Miller, the playwright, though I am insulting the man describing him as such, because everyone knows who he is, and Eugene Gladstone O'Neill's widow, Agnes Boulton and their son, Shane O'Neill. Their daughter, Oona, is married to Charlie Chaplin.

Agnes Boulton is a very interesting person and recently published a book about her life as the wife of Eugene Gladstone O'Neill. I was able to explain to her how her late husband came to be given the name of Gladstone. He was called after William Ewart Gladstone, a British politician and a hypocritical old swine, who, in order to get the Irish vote in the House of Commons in 1886, promised Parnell, the Irish leader, all sorts of reforms and then helped to bring him down for having a love affair, as many people do, with another man's wife – Kitty O'Shea.

Some people refer to Gladstone as the G.O.M., the grand old man, but there is a large section of people who call him the M.O.G., the murderer of Gordon.

However, when Eugene O'Neill was born, Gladstone was a great hero amongst the Irish in America, so his father, who was a very patriotic Irishman, thought this was a good way of showing his patriotism.

With all due respects to James O'Neill, who was a well-known actor in his day, perhaps he was, what Tim Costello once described as, 'a long-distance patriot'.

Another very interesting Irish-American I met at the Hotel Chelsea was Mrs. Elizabeth Gurley Flynn. She has her politics and they are her own and I have no intention of attacking them or praising them, except to say that to be anti-Irish is parallel to being anti-Semitic.

Somebody one time asked Dorothy Thompson what she thought of her compatriots, the American people, and she replied: 'It depends on whether you mean Franklin D. Roosevelt or Al Capone.'

In the same way, when somebody asked me on a television show what I thought of the Irish politically in America, I said: 'It depends on whether you mean the late Senator McCarthy or Mrs. Elizabeth Gurley Flynn.' Both of whom, I may say, are Irish but that is probably the only thing they had in common. This is the only comment I will make on politics.

George Kleinsinger, the composer of *Tubby the Tuba*, and the back-alley opera by the late Don Marquis, *Archie and Mehitabel*, among many other things, has the most marvellous apartment in the Hotel Chelsea.

In addition to playing the piano beautifully, he has in his penthouse apartment a large aquarium of fish, two or three snakes and many birds which fly round on their own in what I can only describe as a tropical forest or something. There are twelve-foot trees and smaller exotic plants which I believe he imports from all over the world. There is also a mynah bird called 'Asia' who floats round and talks and even sings, that is, when he can get a word in edgeways with me. By God, I'll stand no competition from a mynah bird, I can tell you that.

But the mynah bird 'dirtied his bib' as the saying has it in Ireland, because he ate another little bird and he ate everything only the beak; so he had to be institutionalized and put in his cage. In other words, he had to be shoved in the nick. He is now suffering almost life imprisonment, but I think he gets a couple of hours exercise each day.

However, no harm to George Kleinsinger's mynah bird, even if he did commit homicide. There are very few people of my generation all over the world who have not been just as savage, so none of us can afford to talk.

I have to admit though, that the bloody mynah bird bored me after a while, for the simple sufficient reason that its conversation was not altogether comprehensible. I think it spoke with a Twenty-third Street accent.

And speaking of conversation, I remember Tallulah Bankhead telling me that she was at a dinner party once, and she was sitting next to a man who talked during the whole of the meal about ants and this guy gave poor Tallulah a pretty hard time of it. He said: 'Do you know, Miss Bankhead, that ants actually have their own army?'

'Oh,' Tallulah replied, 'is that so? No air force or navy, I presume?'

John Betjeman, the English poet, who is always going round saving the most unlikely looking places such as St. Pancras Station, which to me is not a thing of beauty and a joy for ever, when he next comes to New York, he should go to the Hotel Chelsea. As an *aficionado* of late-Victorian architecture, he would find it very, very impressive. He'd probably write an epic about it.

I was at a party once with John Betjeman's daughter, Candida, and I know a line of a poem which was written about her by an Irish poet when she was a baby:

Candida is one today, what is there for one to say?

At the party also, was the daughter of an English lord. Now an English lord is mainly phoney, in the sense that he has usually got his title about three weeks before for subscribing heavily to the Conservative Party, although I see the Labour Party are getting in on the act too. I wouldn't be surprised if the Reds also get in on it eventually.

However, these two beautiful young ladies were discussing America.

'My daddy hates abroad,' said Candida.

So the lord's daughter – I do not want to sound too theological but she was an honourable or something – agreed with Candida.

George KLEINSINGER at the Chelsea

'My daddy hates abroad too,' she said.

'Does your daddy and Candida's daddy hate the same broad?' I asked her, having a fair command of the New York language. But being an innocent young girl, she did not get my drift.

'I'll tell you something that you may not know,' I continued. 'The American upper classes are quite Anglophile; they are quite pro-English. This is not to say, that when they wanted to get in the vote at the time of "The Troubles" in Ireland, that they were not able to give England hell, secretly, nor, at the time of the Israeli war, that they were not willing enough to be anti-English so as to get in the Jewish vote. But nevertheless, if you want to get on with them, you just ask them what part of England they come from and they will be delighted.'

Neither the lord nor his daughter seemed to like New York very much, though I do not know what New York did on them.

'You tell your lord-daddy,' I said, 'that if he is ever short of a buck, I will take him to a tailors on the corner of Forty-fourth Street not far from the Algonquin Hotel, another excellent institution, and all he will have to do is to sit in the window, wear a white shirt, his old school tie, have a black patch over one eye and smoke one of your horrible English cigarettes in a long holder, and he'll get enough custom from the people who pass, to keep him out of the workhouse.'

We had, for our further comfort on Twenty-third Street, the Oasis saloon, which is also a restaurant. It was owned by Willie Garfinkle, the Lord have mercy on him, for he has recently died, who unfortunately used to close the establishment two hours before the compulsory closing time, which I considered very unfriendly of him.

He was also constantly giving me advice on not to drink anything but beer, which cost fifteen cents a glass, and certainly not to be drinking whiskey, which cost approximately a dollar.

'Listen Willie,' I said to him one day, 'you're supposed to be a Jew in addition to being an American and you are setting a bad example to everybody by trying to screw yourself out of eighty-five cents.'

I think that the 'Oasis' is one of the few places left in the world where you can eat enough off the counter to nearly satisfy your hunger.

Still, the lunch and the dinner are so good, that even the fact that

The late Willie GARFINKLE
2nd the OASIS BAR.
23 street

you've eaten your way through half of the counter, doesn't stop you from going and enjoying your meal. Willie was not all that much of a fool and I wish to God he was with us today. I send Jeannie, his widow, my respects and long may the 'Oasis' prosper under her guidance.

Her staff are so clever that they are actually able to make tea. I don't know whether they use those bloody little bags or not, but the tea is excellent, as of course is the food.

I knew an Irish-American girl who worked in one of Schrafft's restaurants and she told me that she sent a bundle of these tea bags home during the war, at a time when tea was scarce in Ireland. When she went home on holiday, she discovered that her mother had hung them up for Christmas decorations. She didn't know what they were.

Almost next door to the 'Oasis' is the 'Silver Rail' which I don't think was exactly the favourite place of my wife's, nor of Rae Jeffs, a great friend of ours who was staying at the Hotel Chelsea with us.

There was an old Irishman there that I used to meet and he told me that he had been in America since 1916. I did not make the obviously cynical remark that 1916 was a good year to clear out of Ireland.

I asked him what county he came from and because I was standing him a drink, he told me.

Normally if you ask an Irish person where he comes from, except he is from Dublin or Belfast or perhaps Cork City, he is rather reluctant to tell you.

Very few immigrants in New York come from the major cities of other countries and I have yet to meet a Cockney there, although I have met lots of English people. I have never met any Swedes from Stockholm and the only Parisian I know amongst the French colony, is Monsieur Alex of the 'Chateaubriand', a very famous restaurant where I used to eat on my American publisher, Bernard Geis.

I did meet a man from Touraine, however, which is the birthplace of François Rabelais, and he also owns a restaurant off Broadway.

In the same way, there are very few Irishmen from Dublin or Belfast.

Now this is not to say that the New York immigrant is a hick. Actually it is, but I am too hypocritical to say it out straight, but in

SILVER RAIL, 7th AVENUE at 28 street

the second and third generation, they are more American than they are Irish, Polish, Swedish, English, Icelandic or whatever else.

The younger generation in New York are only concerned with being New Yorkers and while, in a sentimental way, I personally am sorry to see the Irish lose their identity, at the same time, they are helping to compose the most exciting city in the world.

The old Irishman in the 'Silver Rail' could hardly be called the younger generation, however.

He told me that he came from Ballyslattery, which is a name I have invented for the reason that I like my health and I do not wish to insult any county in Ireland, north or south.

I knew that the village where this man came from was not exactly the centre of an engineering industry, and I knew that the only piece of machinery he would have been familiar with, would have been a spade for digging potatoes.

To say the least of it, he was not as clever as, shall I say, Robert Kennedy, and he spoke to me in as strong an Irish accent as I have, which was no disgrace to him.

'What did you do when you came to New York first, Mick?' I asked him.

'I made precision instruments for aeroplanes,' he replied.

Well, said I, in my own mind, the guys that went up, during the First World War, in those aeroplanes which were more or less tied together with string, were pretty brave men. But, by God, to go up in a plane that depended on Mick's knowledge of aeronautical engineering, in honour of the poor fellows that he had sent crashing to the ground, I had to give myself a stiff glass of 'Jack Daniels'.

I am extremely fond of swimming and opposite the Hotel Chelsea is the Young Men's Christian Association where I used to swim quite a deal. And they have a rule that you cannot wear bathing trunks and before you dive into the pool, you have to take an ankle bath and you have to take a soap shower.

I asked the attendant the reason for this and he told me that there were so many people coming in to New York from all over the world that they were afraid of the bathing trunks spreading disease. They might have been swimming in some place where there were mosquitos or malaria or God knows what.

Anyway, there was this day when I was with a young Irish fellow and we went across to the Y.M.C.A. together for to have a swim. I regret to say that it was on an 'all male' swimming day, though they do allow women in once or twice a week I think. And next time I am in New York, I must find out about the rules and regulations for the lady swimmers.

But this Irish fellow went up to the pool with his trunks on. Now he was the father of three fine children, and, if you get my meaning, I am sure he had nothing to be ashamed of, when he was stripped.

'Look,' I said, 'you can't wear trunks here.'

So he turned round and went back to his locker and the next thing I knew, he was putting his clothes back on.

'Why don't you want to go in undressed?' I said. 'There is nobody here except other blokes and, without being too personal, you do not look as if you have anything to be ashamed of in the nude.'

'Yes, I have,' he answered. 'It makes me look so skinny.'

I have an invitation to use the excellent swimming pool of the Young Men's Hebrew Association on Lexington Avenue, any time I like, and when I was over that side of New York, I would go in and have a swim.

I was standing in the showers one day and a little Negro boy came in and looked at me.

'Hiya, Mr. Behan,' he said. 'You are wanted on the telephone.'

'Oh, thanks,' I said, 'but will you come down with me to the locker room while I put some clothes on and then you can show me where the telephone is.'

So I wrapped a towel round myself and we went downstairs. As I was putting on my clothes, the thought struck me.

'Listen, young fellow,' I said. 'How did you know me? Did you see me on the television?'

'No, sir.'

'Surely you don't go to the theatre on Broadway?'

'No, sir.'

'Did you see my photograph in the newspapers?'

'No, sir.'

'Then how the hell did you know I was myself?'

'Well, sir. I saw you in the showers with the other men and I knew Behan was not a Jewish name.'

To a certain extent, this American custom of not wearing bathing costumes disturbed me, not because I am shy about naked swimming, but other people noticed that I was not a Hebrew. It would not disturb me now, however, because that little matter has been rectified, if a little late in life.

There is another excellent swimming pool, which I have an invitation to use any time I am in Brooklyn, at the St. George Hotel and peculiarly enough, it is a salt water pool. As I say, there is everything in New York.

The extreme modesty of the American beaches surprised me. You cannot go down on the beach, take off your clothes, put on your bathing costume, get into the water and have a swim. You must either take your clothes off in a car, or in compartments specially provided, at a fee.

Some cynical Americans have told me that the shockability of the beach police depends on the warmth of their friendship with the owners of the bathing undressing establishments.

There are some wonderful beaches outside of New York, though I can only speak from personal experience of two of them. Those at Coney Island and those at Fire Island.

Coney Island, like a great number of things in New York, is hard to compare with any place else. It is a terrific, fabulous and an extremely proletarian institution – I hope I don't offend the State Department – where thousands upon thousands of ordinary folk get out on the subway for fifteen cents and thoroughly enjoy themselves. I would say they enjoyed themselves as much as the class of people who are able to go to Las Vegas.

Now I am not knocking Las Vegas for I was in the place and I hope to go there again. One of the vices I haven't got however, is gambling. I left having neither won a cent nor lost a cent.

Coney Island has got everything except, oddly enough, hard liquor. But you can get any amount of beer and frankfurters, which I cordially detest. It is almost a New York in itself. There is a steeplechase, a huge swimming pool, a restaurant, places where the children play, games for them to enjoy, and there is even a place for older people to sit down and have a look at the younger ones disporting themselves in the pool.

Coney Island is almost a microcosm.

The pleasures of Fire Island are for a very different class of person and I would say you would have to be pretty wealthy to be able to rent one of the shacks there during the season. The cost for a bed alone, with nothing to eat or drink, is twenty-five dollars a night, which is over eight pounds.

But it is a beautiful island and the beaches are nothing but sand.

I am told that tremendous damage is done each year by fire, for all, or nearly all the houses are built of wood. I suppose the owners of them have to get back the cost of rebuilding somehow.

I was there one time with my wife and we left on the Long Island railroad from the late Pennsylvania Station, which as far as I could see, was practically a department store. I mean, you could go on a shopping spree, have some food and a drink, and even go to the toilet.

I say even go to the toilet, because it is an interesting aspect of American puritanism, that New York City at any rate, lacks the civilized amenities of even the smaller European towns. And stranger still is the fact that you can buy nude women on playing cards and other interesting things of this sort on Broadway, but no toilet facilities are available there if you wish to browse amongst them for several hours at a time.

The trip by train is about an hour or so and then there is the ferry ride across to Fire Island. On this day, there were quite a few people on the boat and one of them came over and started talking to us. He was a blond American chap called Don, and he told us that he made this trip two or three times a year, in season. He seemed rather reluctant to say exactly what he did, which is no harm to him. I am rather reluctant to say what I do.

Anyway when we got to the Island, I discovered there were no roads. There were only little boardwalks which were just large enough for the school bus and the fire engine to use. I saw no other form of transport at all, unless you'd be wanting to call the colourful little wagons the people pull, transport.

We walked a few steps to the Pines Boatel where we were staying, and we were given a great meal and a great welcome. Afterwards a crowd of fellows came in and played the juke box and they began doing a dance which they continued to do by the hour.

My wife told me it was the Madison, or mad something. Actually, I found it very interesting because I had not seen it done before and after a jar or two, I started dancing the damn thing myself.

Later that evening, somebody asked me if I was a homosexual, because apparently Cherry Grove, a part of the Island near to where we were staying, was a sort of haven for these fellows.

Now I think that people have much more to trouble them than how adults behave. I am of course of the opinion, like every reasonable man, that any kind of sex with any sort of interference with kids, of say under fourteen, should be prohibited by law.

There is no point in talking about homosexuality as if it were a disease. I've seen people with homosexuality and I've seen people with tuberculosis and there is no similarity at all.

My attitude to homosexuality is rather like that of the woman who, at the time of the trial of Oscar Wilde, said she didn't mind what they did, so long as they didn't do it in the street and frighten the horses.

I think everyone agrees that with young people it is a bad thing for society, but amongst consenting adults, it is entirely their own affair.

Anyway, I joined these fellows and they taught me the Madison. I remember we were at a party afterwards in this very modern house, all glass, and one of the few houses I saw that was not built of wood.

Don, the American chap, was with us and he asked me to sing a few rebel songs in his honour, which I did, though I don't think he knew any more about the history of Ireland than I do about the man from Mars. However, we were all enjoying ourselves, until Don falls off his chair and sits on my glass of brandy which I had left on the floor, and the glass breaks into tiny little pieces.

'Are you sure you haven't damaged yourself?' I said.

'No,' he said. 'I think I am all right.' And I looked down on the floor and my blood of life seemed to have disappeared in the blood from his bottom.

The following morning he told me that he had had to go to the doctor and have two stitches put in his backside.

Cherry Grove. Fire Island

'You won't forget the night you met the Behans, anyhow,' I said.

One of the pure pleasures of my life was walking along the beach to Cherry Grove. It was a lovely, lovely sunny day and you could nearly have swum in the sea, even though it was late in September.

An extraordinary thing I noticed about Fire Island, was the absence of Negroes. I don't know whether the word 'Negro' is the right one or not; some people call them 'coloured' and I've heard Negroes themselves referring to each other just as 'blacks'.

Whether it is that the Negroes cannot afford the luxuries of Fire Island, or whether it is simply racial prejudice, I do not know.

My racial prejudices are practically nil. I say practically, because sometimes when I read about the famine in Ireland or the Easter Week Rising, I may get a bit bitter against England and the English.

I am against the partition of Ireland and I do not think it is good for the people of England that they should occupy other people's countries.

It is certainly not good for the people of Ireland, because it prevents us having any real politics. All our politics are concentrated on the border which divides Ireland. When I was in prison in England, I thought the English should clear out of Ireland and I think so now. If somebody should ask me for to clear out the Irish playwrights from the West End, then I would tell them that we are thinking of that as a reprisal.

On the other hand, I have one brother married to an English girl; I have a sister married to a Scots boy and another brother is married to a Scots girl.

The principal thing to do in this world, is to get something to eat and something to drink and somebody to love you.

There are three dominant Harlems in New York: Italian, Puerto Rican, and Negro Harlem. I was not a whole lot in the last named, but I wish I could have been there before 1958 when the Savoy Ballroom disappeared. I believe it was the most fantastic place, where you could learn jazz, have a drink or two and see a colourful spectacle. It is sad that the wonderful desegregation that is taking place in New York had to come at the expense of places like these.

I was in Harlem one time and I stopped to listen to a speaker at Saint Nicholas Terrace.

Naturally, I did not expect that everybody would know the differ-

RiiS BEACH, ROCKAWAYS

ence between an Irishman, a Manxman, a Welshman, a Scotsman or an Englishman. But at the same time, I would have expected them to know that I didn't come from Birmingham in Alabama. Some of the crowd, I am sorry to say, though I suppose perfectly understandably, seemed to think that one white person was much the same as another. And I think some of them thought that I was a spy for the Ku Klux Klan.

Now I have read a great deal about the Black Muslims, and I saw some of them because they were pointed out to me, and they were highly respectably dressed young men. I can understand them telling the Negroes that, under no circumstances should they buy from anywhere else except a Negro store, even if the goods cost a few cents more. And I would say that for the Negro merchants, the Black Muslims must be quite a good deal.

I know in its early days, the Sinn Fein movement in Ireland was very much encouraged, even by pro-British merchants and shopkeepers, because it stipulated that everyone should buy Irish goods, which was perhaps a good idea. But on the other hand, I know that some of the people who subscribed to Sinn Fein, wouldn't have agreed with its other objective; to have a free Ireland.

Of course the colour problem is a worldwide one. It is nonsense to say that it is merely an American one. What happens in America is of great interest to people all over the world.

The Irish are seldom anti-Negro, but then the Irish do not enter into economic competition. There are thousands of Negroes in Dublin, but they're all Chief's sons, and they're usually attending the Universities and are not lining up for a job in competition with the natives.

The idea of returning hate for hate in some ways I understand, except that some of us are inclined to do it with the wrong people.

I remember once in Paris, a very famous Negro author whom I know, was holding forth at a table in the Boulevard St. Germain about the sufferings of the Negroes in America. I was with a friend of mine at the time, who had no racial prejudices whatsoever. His principal prejudices were in favour of lay and liquor, strangely enough in that order, because reversed they would not make a lot of sense. At least, I think any girl would say so.

However, my friend was the only white person present apart

HARLEM - Saturday morning

from myself and both he and I sympathized with everything the
Negro writer was saying. In a sense, he was preaching to the con-
verted: he was shoving an open door. Of course I am sorry for
the Negroes in America, though I don't agree at all times with
them. I do not agree with persecuting anybody.

Now I don't think the French have a lot to shout about over
Algeria, and the Germans most certainly do not have a lot to shout
about over the atrocities to six million Jews during the last war. I
think every nationality has persecuted somebody at some time or another. It would do well for the Irish to remember that Saint Patrick
was brought over to Ireland by the Irish after the slave raid, and
arrived there first as a slave.

But all the while this Negro author was talking, the assembled
company kept staring at my friend. When he had finished, more
from the want of breath than from anything else, my friend,
looking round from the glares of the rest of the company, said to
him: 'I am proud to know you. You certainly seem to feel the
sufferings of the Negroes very, very, much.'

'Why shouldn't I,' said the writer. 'Aren't I a Negro myself?'

'Oh, I'm sorry,' said my friend. 'I hadn't realized.'

I was on Saint Nicholas Avenue one time and I stopped in the street
to buy a newspaper. The old lady who was selling them said to me:
'Now I hope you are behaving yourself, Brendan.' So my fame had
extended to Harlem.

I was also in the Baby Grand Club with Frank Fields, the Negro
composer, where there was one of the finest comedians I have ever
heard in my life, Nipsey Russell.

Sometimes I feel that the Irish and the English comedian, and for
the matter of that, the Negro and the Jewish, depend upon private
jokes of their own. Nipsey's jokes were of an international quality;
that is to say, if you were not bringing your aunt to the show. And
some of his gags were so funny that I started writing them down for
the purpose of telling them to other people.

Nipsey looked down and saw what I was doing.

'There's Brendan Behan,' he said, 'writing down my gags so as he
can use them as his own in *The Hostage*.' I met him afterwards and
he is a most charming and intelligent person.

Later on that evening, Frank and I went to a rather swish sort of club where, apart from myself, they were all Negroes, but they were Negroes with a difference. I mean, although they gave me a great welcome, I don't think, had I been a subway worker, even a black one, they would have been exactly pleased to meet me.

I was introduced to one man who said he was the first Negro on the New York Stock Exchange. Now I have met people on the New York Stock Exchange before and I knew a fellow who gave me a tip one time, which unfortunately I did not use because I know nothing about it at all.

To tell the honest truth, I do not find financiers terribly exciting at the best of times, whether they are black or white; Catholics, Protestants, Jews, Lutherans, Atheists or any other religion. I suppose it is because they are in a different racket from me.

'Where in the name of God are we?' I asked Frank Fields. 'What kind of people are these? I'm not so foolish as to expect black people to be singing spirituals or dancing and entertaining all the time, but this place reminds me of the Irish Club in London.'

'You've often heard the expression "fat cats", Brendan,' he said.

'Sure,' I said. 'It means people who have got a lot of money.'

'That's right,' Frank replied, 'and these are "fat black cats".'

And talking of the Irish Club in London, they were holding classes there one time in the Irish language, which apparently some of its members wished to learn. I had met two Irish labourers in a public house across the street from the club who spoke practically nothing else but Irish. And I had the temerity to ask them up to the club to say a few words to the people at the classes, so they would know the true Irish language accent.

Actually the best way to get a proper accent in either the Irish or the Hebrew language, is to go to Central Park on a cold winter's morning and listen to a taxi-man clearing his throat.

But that is not the only reason for going to Central Park. There are all sorts of amusements there, some of which are free. There is a carousel, pony rides, things to eat and even a small zoo. I am not suggesting that it is anything like the Bronx Zoo, which is a marvellous place, though I have yet to see a finer zoo than the one in the

Phoenix Park in my own native city. And to this day, lions are bred there which are exported to zoos all over the world.

But in a certain part of the Bronx Zoo many of the animals run freely about together, rather on the lines of Whipsnade Zoo in England. It is a very impressive sight and I would think George Kleinsinger must be charmed with the bird section, and they once had a fiercesome-looking taipan snake, which was apparently the only known one of its kind in America, until it went to where all good snakes go when they die.

> I brought me mot up to the Zoo
> For to show her the lion and the kangaroo . . .

And if you are thinking of taking her to the Children's Zoo in the Bronx, let me give you some advice. Beg, borrow or steal a child, because no grown-up is allowed in without one.

CONEY ISLAND

PARACHUTE RIDE, CONEY ISLAND

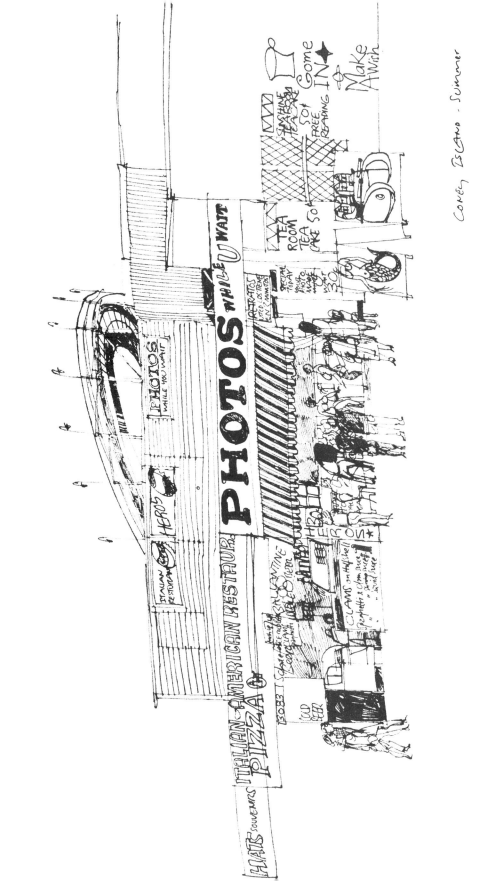

Coney Island - Summer

CONEY ISLAND - WINTER

NATHAN'S, CONEY ISLAND

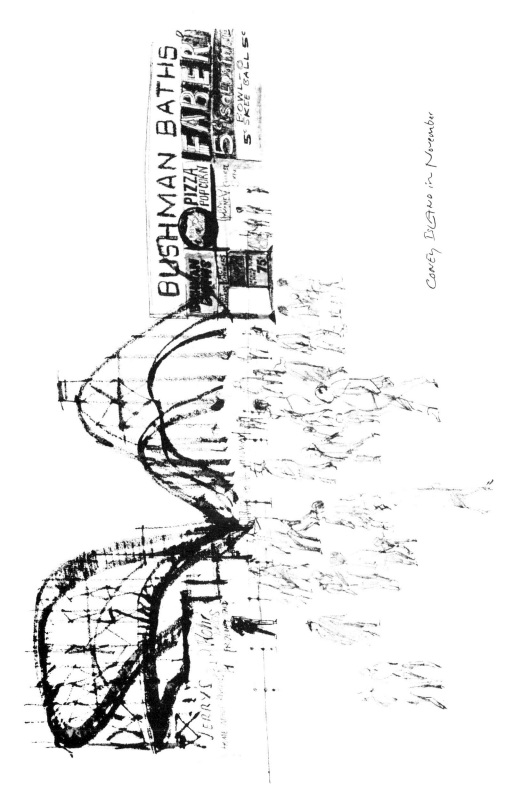

Coney Island in November

The Coney Island Elevated Railway

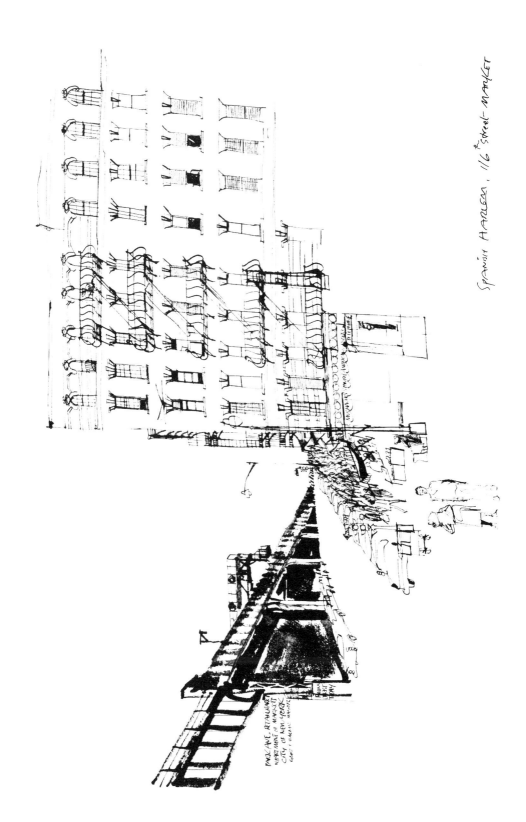

SPANISH HARLEM, 116th Street MARKET

PARK AVE. RETAIL MARKET
DEPARTMENT OF MARKETS
CITY OF NEW YORK
ROBERT F. WAGNER, MAYOR

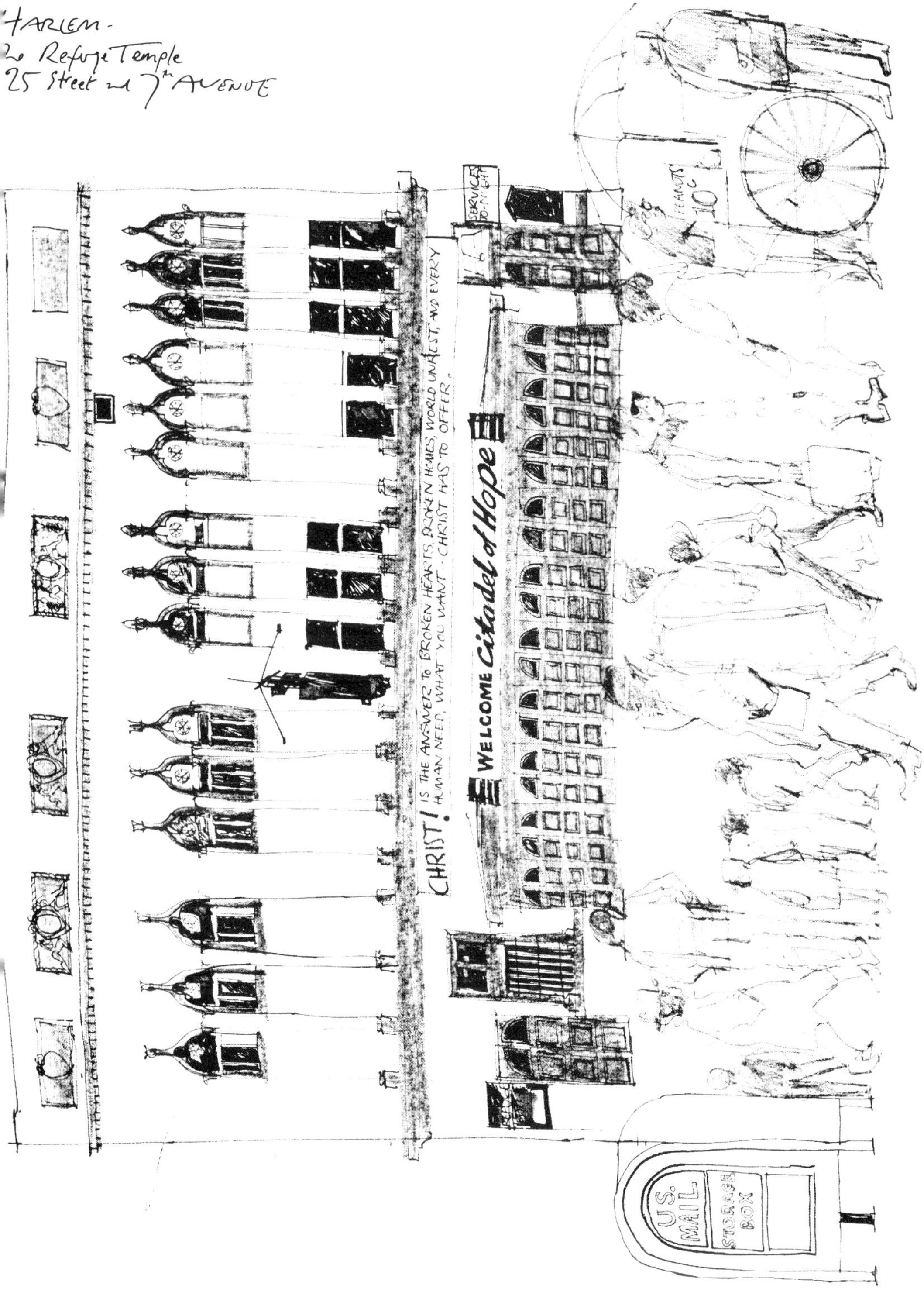

HARLEM —
The Refuge Temple
125 Street and 7th AVENUE

CHRIST! IS THE ANSWER to BROKEN HEARTS, BROKEN HOMES, WORLD UNREST, and EVERY HUMAN NEED. WHAT YOU WANT, CHRIST HAS TO OFFER.

WELCOME Citadel of Hope

SERVICE TO-NIGHT

PEANUTS 10¢

U.S. MAIL STORAGE BOX

Central Park Carriages

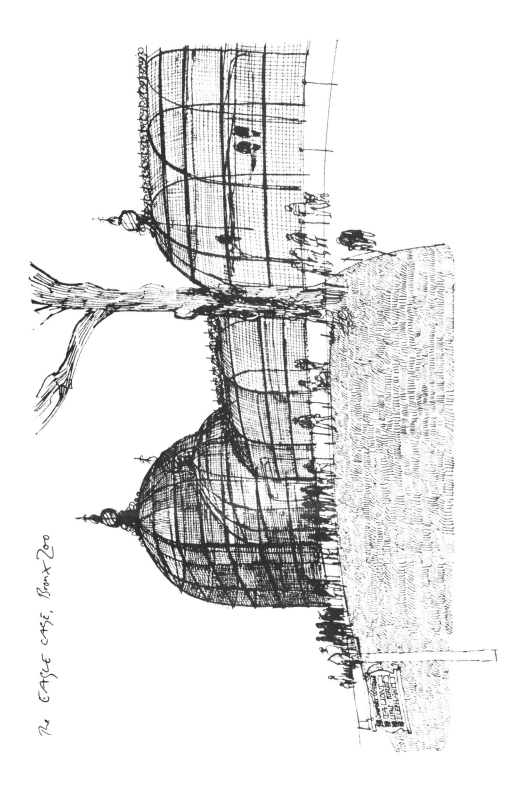

The EAGLE CAGE, Bronx Zoo

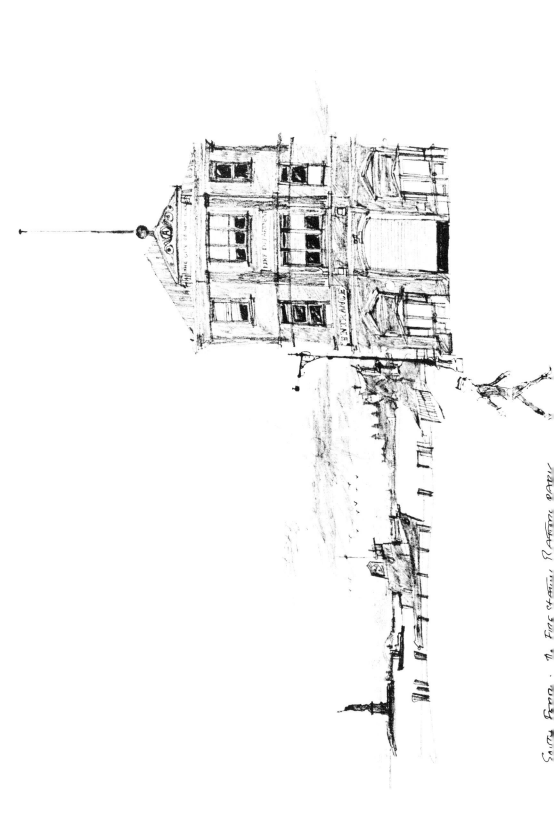

SOUTH FRONT - The FIVE STATION, PLATFORM, PARIS

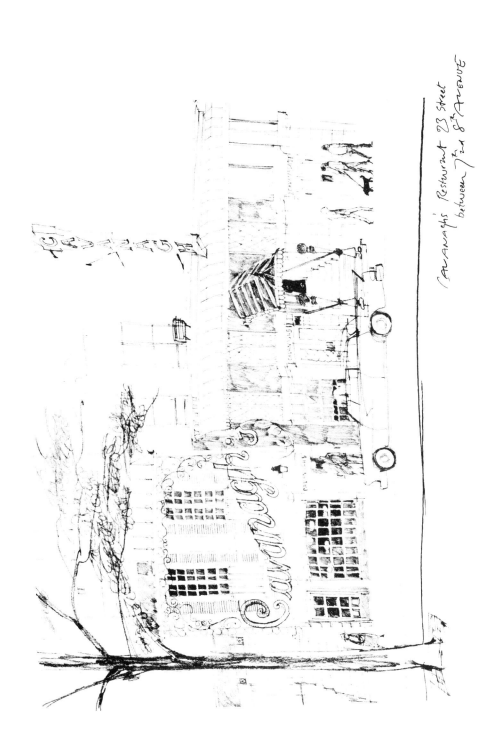

Cavanagh's Restaurant 23 Street
between 7th & 8th Avenue

The Fiesta of San Gennaro, Lower East Side

Beats, Boweryites and Chinamen

The famous Greenwich Village is the only genuine Latin Quarter left in either Western Europe or any place else that I know. It is reputedly full of involved sex, and of course there is vice there.

There is vice in London and there is vice in Paris, and in Reykjavik and in East Jesus, Kansas. You can get vice anywhere, but the only exciting thing I found in the Village was when some fellow offered me a smoke of marijuana.

Unfortunately, the poor old marijuana had to struggle against a couple of bottles of bourbon, so I cannot tell much about that.

There are phonies there too, phoney-phonies, although I don't believe anybody is utterly a phoney. To hell with it, I never found a phoney who wasn't willing to stand a struggling artist a drink if he had the price of one, so he has got his function like everyone else.

And there is a definite loyalty in the Village that extends right through the Italian housewife rearing her family, through the Irish docker to the artists, whether phoney or not.

Of course people out in the bogs and in suburbia all over the world, like to be horrified by the recreational activities of artists, although I understand, in a book called *Peyton Place*, that the *bourgeoisie* – or the 'booboisie', as H. L. Mencken called them – didn't do too badly themselves.

There is the Italian quarter where they hold, every September, the Feast of San Gennaro and this really is a feast. People come from Harlem, from Chinatown and from all over the place to see it, and the crowds are so thick that any form of dancing would be out of the question.

However, there is food in plenty and a little gambling, though I don't think you could make much money at it, for San Gennaro was a poor saint. He was also an agnostic one, so he doesn't embarrass anybody with his miracles and the like.

If you want to go to Mass, there is St. Anthony's church, the Franciscan church, which has a hall where the kids go and play basketball while their girl friends sit around and cheer them on, occasionally in very un-Franciscan prose. However, the Franciscans don't mind that. They do great work for all the boys and girls in the Village.

Some of the bars are quite famous. There is the 'White Horse', which was the favourite drinking place of Dylan Thomas, and O' Henry's Steak House where Norman Mailer goes when he comes over to the Village. He has a house in Brooklyn Heights and he organized a party there for Saint Patrick's Day, which I could nearly tell all about, but I say nearly because, well, it was a pretty good party.

Then there is 'Chumley's' on Bedford Street and 'Stefan's' on Christopher Street, where I understand the barman one time was not very complimentary about me as a man, although he liked my plays. No harm to him. He is entitled to his opinions, the same as everybody else.

I was in 'Ricky's' one time where I met the late Franz Kline, who as far as I know was a very good painter. He invited me to his studio, which was in the Village. I suppose they will be shoving up a plaque to him on the wall of his house, though you have got to give them ten years to get round to it.

The centre of activities is in Washington Square, which is a beautiful little square with Georgian houses that rather resemble the architecture of my native city. There is also a *petit* Arc de Triomphe, which is called the Washington Arch, and there are magnificent trees and, what they call in Brooklyn, the 'boids'. I haven't heard them speak like that to be truthful, but perhaps, because I speak like that myself, I do not notice it.

Some of the most exciting plays are to be found in the Village, such as Jack Gelber's *The Connection*, and Jean Genet's *The Blacks*, and I also have to remind myself that I had two off-Broadway productions there. *The Quare Fellow* was produced by Jose Quintero at 'The Circle in the Square', which is one of the most famous theatres in the world, and *The Hostage* was produced at 'One Sheridan Square', by Perry Bruskin, who lives in a very nice house, but far away from Manhattan Island.

There are also film shows that you would not ordinarily see up town.

If you are interested in folk-singing, Washington Square on a Sunday must be unique. Folk-singers I personally detest. I would shoot every one of them, because I am a singer myself – at least I was until my larynx gave in to too many cigarettes. And they always tell a pack of lies. They get an old banjo in their hands and they call themselves folk-singers. Now my uncle wrote plenty of Irish songs, and I also learnt songs off my mother, who has never stopped singing. Not even the Depression could stop her. I can sing in Irish and in English and I've had an odd stab at singing in French, but I never knew I was a folk-singer.

I will admit however, that some of these pseudo-folk-singers seem to be excellent composers, but most of them will never admit that they haven't written the song themselves.

I wrote a song about Michael Collins. He was the Commander-in-Chief of the Free State Army of Ireland which accepted the Treaty with England, and against whom my father fought. Politically I did not agree with him either, though the poor chap was killed about six months before I was born. But I wrote a song about him and I used a Gaelic air. I think it is a good song, but unfortunately I am not able to sing it, not alone on account of my throat, but because I can never remember anything that I write myself.

I will have forgotten this book long before you have paid your money for it, I can assure you. Singing your own songs or reading your own work, to me is a form of mental incest.

I don't care whether these fellows are black or white, or whether they are singing about God, or about the sufferings of the fishermen in San Salerno, or about the oyster pickers at Chesapeake or Sheepshead Bay, or whatever it's called, if they want to sing, they should just sing and there's an end on it. They do not have to call themselves folk-singers.

If I was a young man and single, I think I would suffer these goddam whiners and moaners and mandolin twangers and I would advise other young men to do the same. I would put up with the fellow with a beard – no harm wearing a beard for this is the mark of the trade – and I would put up with the girls with their Mona Lisa hair styles, and I would put up with sitting on the floor. (I think they burn the chairs in the place because apparently they don't feel that a chair is the proper place to sit when listening to one of these groaners.)

But there are always some lovely girls sitting round, either on the grass or on the floor, who look reverently up at the latest importation from the Appalachian Mountains singing his songs. If she is too engrossed in looking up at the banjo-twanger on the stage, he can always be shot down by whispering in her ear that the fellow is a homosexual.

If this fails, you can always go off and buy yourself a bloody mandolin, and even if you come from the Lower East Side of New York, you can always change your accent a little bit and say you come from Kentucky. No harm to Kentucky of course. I will leave it at the point, that it is well worth your while sitting amongst these young ladies.

Anyway, the younger generation from all over the world have decided that the Village is the place and I think they are right. I know I drank a great deal of wine in it.

I suppose the Latin Quarter in Paris, at one stage of the game, was similar to the Village, in the days when Sylvia Beach owned a famous bookshop there. She was a New Yorker, a very noble woman and a great credit to the human race, and she loved New York, but she loved it in the same way as I love Dublin, from a distance. Three thousand miles away, in fact. She was also the first person to publish the works of James Joyce who was in Paris at the time.

CHUMLEY'S BAR
GREENWICH VILLAGE

He sent a play of his, called *Exiles*, to the Theatre de l'Œuvre but it was returned to him. 'Mr. Joyce,' the rejection slip read, 'we have just fought a World War and there are a lot of widows and orphans as a result. We think your play a bit too sad.'

'I suppose I should have given Richard a cork leg to jolly things up a bit,' Joyce remarked bitterly to Sylvia Beach, and he put the play aside and went on writing *Ulysses* which he had nearly finished.

Now I think that a bit of jollying-up does no harm, so I have decided to call my next play, *Richard's Cork Leg*.

Also in Paris with James Joyce, was Ernest Hemingway, Scott Fitzgerald, Gertrude Stein and her friend Alice B. Toklas, and many other writers. I know a couple of rather irreverent lines about Gertrude Stein's autobiography, which she wrote as the life of Alice B. Toklas:

'I absolutely must decline,
To dance in the streets for Gertrude Stein,
And as for Alice B. Tok-er-las,
I'd sooner Shakespeare and a bloody big box of choc-er-lates'

However all these writers moved to France and many of them settled there. A lot of people like to think that Paris was never the same as it was in those days, but as Hemingway remarked to a friend of mine, he heard tell the same story in 1920, that Paris was not the same as it had been in 1910.

They are certainly saying this about the Village now, but it is a much more exciting place than the Boulevard St. Germain or Soho, though the divil a much I ever saw in Soho. It does not compare with the Village in any way; it compares with the Village in the same way as a bottle of American beer compares with a bottle of champagne.

I met Allen Ginsberg, the poet, in the Village, and he introduced me to another poet who gets one hundred dollars a month from Uncle Sam for being mad. In Ireland, a poet has to do it for nothing.

But Allen Ginsberg is a very interesting and important man. He wrote a wonderful book of verse with an even more wonderful title: *Howl.*

We had a very good lunch together in a Jewish restaurant and I like Jewish food once I'm not in the company of what I call a Sinn Fein Jew, who will order you all sorts of exotic delicacies just to show off, and certainly not the kind of food he would eat at home, himself.

I believe it comes from the Yemenites and, in my opinion, it ought to go back to the Yemenites. I've no doubt they look well enough on it and it enables them to build roads, but it doesn't suit a transatlantic showman like myself.

The most controversial person I met in the Village was Jack Kerouac, the novelist. Although he did not live there, he would come over quite often to meet his friends, have a drink and try to take the micky out of visiting Irish playwrights, which I may say he did not find a very profitable occupation. But he is a sturdy-looking chap and I'd sooner take a cigarette from him than a punch on the mouth. And he is a professional writer the same as myself.

I remember being introduced to Thornton Wilder by Jim Thurber.

'Listen, Thornton,' Jim said, 'I want you to meet Brendan Behan.'

'Oh, sure. I know Brendan Behan. I recognize him,' replied Thornton Wilder.

'I can only recognize his voice,' said poor Jim, because at the time he was nearly blind. 'Let us all sit down and have a drink, Thornton,' he said. 'Brendan is like ourselves; he's an old pro.'

Now in England it wouldn't be exactly complimentary to call someone this.

'Jesus, what the hell do you mean, I'm an old pro?' I asked.

So Jim explained to me that he meant a professional writer.

Apart from being a professional writer, and a good one, Jack Kerouac invented the term 'beatnik', and how he came to invent it, I will explain.

When he was beginning to become well-known, the reporters arrived to interview him.

'Now Mr. Kerouac, what would you call your generation? All those writers who went to Paris after the First World War, they were known as the "Lost Generation". Have you a name for your own?'

'I don't know anything about generations,' said Kerouac, 'except fathers and mothers and uncles and aunts. What do you mean? I just eat and drink and discuss writing and painting or anything else I happen to be interested in.'

'Look, Mr. Kerouac, you have got to give us something. Our readers want it. You are a writer and so are we.'

'All right,' said Kerouac, 'I'm the Beat Generation.'

So when the first sputnik went up, the word became 'Beatnik.'

Anybody who has ever seen a side view of me knows that I am not 'a square,' but I think the beatniks are highly dangerous men. They are all after a job and they're dangerous. I don't mind people going after a job, but the job that the beatnik is after is my job.

There is nothing that annoys me more than people who try to put a tag on generations of writers, as if all writing was done in a maternity hospital. In the name of God, writers do not come in generations.

Somebody asked me once, if I was a working-class writer. Now I am most definitely of working-class origin but I do not consider myself a working-class writer, or an Irish writer, or any other kind of specialized sect. I just consider myself a writer.

'You go and ask Evelyn Waugh if he is a middle-class writer,' I said, 'and if he says he is, then I will be a working-class writer.'

Now I have the greatest and highest respect for Mr. Waugh's prose, despite his antics with top hats and ascot vests and big ear phones. I'm sure he could afford to buy smaller ones, but he just won't. Still, he is a marvellous writer and I don't know of anybody, other than Waugh, who could have written a sentence like this: 'His chin was so prominent that when he was eating, the crumbs that fell from his lips were not permanently lost to him.'

He has his antics as I have mine, and if he knows anything about me – which perhaps he does – probably my antics are as reprehensible to him.

Michael MacLiammoir, the famous Irish actor, once wrote in a newspaper that it was a pity that Irish writers were not more cohesive. He was referring to myself and Samuel Beckett, who is an old and very dear friend of mine and a marvellous playwright. I don't know what his plays are about, but I know I enjoy them. I do not know what a swim in the ocean is about, but I enjoy it. I enjoy the water flowing over me.

I don't see why a writer should be cohesive, any more than plumbers or bankers should be cohesive.

Father Tom Fox, a priest who writes very excellent documents, even if they happen to be a bit depressing for a sinner like myself to read, told me that the one thing he hated in a restaurant was to be seated beside another priest.

But writers are cohesive in that they happen to like each other's company to the extent that they feel another writer is the only person worth while discussing their work. Except for the money, of course. As Dr. Johnson said, the man that writes and doesn't do it for money is a blockhead.

I hope this answer satisfies Michael MacLiammoir. He had a marvellous show on Broadway, *The Importance of Being Oscar*, which I saw at a matinee on Saint Patrick's Day, which was my way of cele-

Montague Terrace, Brooklyn Heights

brating the day, because it was extracts from the writings of a great Irish dramatist by a great Irish actor.

And while I am on the subject of Michael MacLiammoir, my mother was sent by my granny, one time, for nine-penny pig's cheek.

Such a thing at the price, was not easily come by, even twenty-five years ago. But anyway, in the heels of the reels, Mr. Hug Melinn of Dorset Street, as then was, dug up a cheek which he was willing to part with at the price mentioned.

The poor cheek had been squeezed up against the side of the barrel, which twisted his jaw and gave his one eye a most alarming squint.

My mother looked at it for a moment and ventured to say to the shopman, 'Mr. Hug, that's a very peculiar looking cheek.'

'And what,' asks Mr. Hug, 'do you expect for ninepence – MeHail Mock Lallamore?'

I beg his indulgence.

Begging in the Bowery is a recognized occupation. I went down there on occasion and I am put in the invidious position of telling how I came to go there, at the same time making myself out almost like St. Francis of Assisi.

Now I identify myself with 'the-down-and-outs' not that I wish to be one of them, but because being down and out is being lonely and segregated, even among the lonely. If I were skint, I would sooner be skint on the Bowery than in Westchester County. It is more civilized and the conversation is better, but I would prefer the Algonquin or the Hotel Chelsea to either place.

Before I went down to the Bowery, I used to get change from the bank. There are as many banks in New York as there are churches in Dublin, although there are more churches over in Brooklyn than in any other place I know. It is called 'The City of the Churches'.

But in the bank I would change a few dollars into quarters and I used to give them to the guys who asked me for it, for the price of a cup of coffee. Most of them were not doing so well.

And I met a policeman of Norwegian extraction who asked me if I would like to go around the place with him. The idea of going round as a sort of social, or sociable worker, didn't exactly appeal to me.

'That's all right,' the cop said. 'The boys will know you. They have seen your photograph in the paper and they will almost expect you to come down and live with them.'

Now I've lived in worse places. I remember sleeping out in Hyde Park and only having one penny. And I went into a lavatory – not for the purpose of using it, for as I had not eaten for a couple of days, there was no need – but for to wash my feet, for they were very sore and hot. I flushed the toilet a couple of times and then when the water was quite clean, I took off my socks and shoes and I put my feet in it. I flushed the toilet again, first on one foot, and then on the other. I sat there for some time afterwards, because fortunately someone had left a newspaper, and I fell asleep in the place.

The idea that you can walk up to any policeman, in either England or Ireland, and ask him for a bed for the night at the police station is not true in my experience. The only place I know of where this did happen was in the Channel Islands, where a friend of mine got a bed in the police station for two nights. On the third night he was told that if he was not gone off the island by that day, he would be up before the judge in the morning for vagrancy, and would be getting, not alone a bed for the night, but for many days as well.

'A fellow-feeling makes us wondrous kind,' in the words of Shakespeare, but then Shakespeare said pretty well everything, and what he left out, James Joyce put in.

I would be a bigger hypocrite than I am, if I were to say that all police officers are angels, but in a great number of cases in the Bowery, they were.

I went with this policeman of Norwegian extraction into a boarding-house where he said he had an errand to do. There was an old man lying on a bed and he had his wooden leg propped up at the end of it. The cop took out a packet of cigarettes and handed him a few, and he also handed him a watch. 'There you are, Poppa,' he said. Before we left, I saw him slip his hand into his pocket and give the old fellow some change.

Out in the street I asked the officer about the watch.

'Well,' he said, 'he gives me his watch in case somebody would pinch it from him in the course of the night, and I give it back to him each morning. Sometimes I help him on with his wooden leg if there isn't anyone else around to do it.'

Though I certainly would not recommend the Bowery, there are people living there who are not derelicts and who lead quite ordinary lives and go out to work every morning and have their own apartments. These may not be similar to the Waldorf-Astoria in New York or Claridges in London or the Georges Cinque in Paris, but they are family apartments, and as such they're all right.

I'm afraid there are plenty of others who, as in every large city, sleep on the floor, or as the Cockney calls it, on the 'Rory O'Moore'. These people are congenital 'down-and-outs' like myself, in the sense that they are not prepared to do an honest day's work. I hasten to add that the only person I ever knew in Ireland to refuse honest employment at trade union rates, is myself. I did work once, for six weeks at a stretch, on the building of a new hospital in the Phoenix Park in Dublin, which is not very far from the American Embassy. It is one of the finest buildings I know, and is certainly in one of the finest settings. As the American government were the first to recognize the Irish Free State when it was established in 1922, they were able to pick the best part of the city for their Embassy.

Many of the people on the Bowery are simply unfortunate in the sense that they have absolutely no skill, but some of these fellows believe that they are artists. The truth is that they are half-arsed artists, and they have utterly no talent in the world, but God in Heaven and the Archangel Gabriel would not be able to drive this fact into their heads.

Others are genuine alcoholics. I remember discussing with Leonard Lyons, a certain film actress who attributed her fall from stardom to alcoholism.

'Well, Brendan,' said Leonard, 'her fall wasn't so great, because first of all, she wasn't so high a star as she makes out and secondly, she wasn't as low a drunk as she makes out.'

To be an alcoholic is not such a good deal, I can tell you, but if you haven't got the money to buy decent liquor, it must be crucifixion altogether.

I first learnt the use of whiskey at the age of six from my grandmother, who said: 'Give him the sup of it now, and he will never know the taste of it when he grows up,' which, I suppose, is the biggest understatement of all time; in my case anyway.

Bowery Bar

But these chaps simply drink what they can afford. There is a certain vile concoction called 'Red Biddy' which is sold legally most places in the world. People have told me in Ireland that it is very good for a cold if you boil it up and put sugar in it. But the quantities which these chaps are inclined to consume would knock even me out, and they become so addicted to this particular kind of fire-water, that they prefer it to everything else.

I was with a genuine alcoholic in the Bowery one time, and I could see he was in a bad way for a drink, as I've often been myself, and I offered him one.

'I would give the two eyes in my head for a drink,' he said, and as his two eyes didn't look such a hot proposition, I did not altogether fancy the transaction. However, I took him into a bar and I was going to give him a large glass of bourbon, and myself a cup of tea. In the wonderful spring air of New York, I was off the drink at the time, and I had a show on Broadway and I was doing television work. Altogether the day was too full for to bother about liquor. Also the ordinary New Yorker, whether working-class, middle-class or upper-class, hasn't a deal of time for what he describes as 'a lush', which is a man who drinks to excess. Ordinarily, I am a 'lush' but I wasn't a 'lush' at this particular time. I was a 'lush' on leave, shall I say.

But this other guy I was with was a 'lush' on the Bowery and I felt for him as I would feel for myself. It was almost as if I were looking in a mirror. I certainly did not feel like a member of some charitable organization.

'No, thanks,' he said, 'just give me the money for a whiskey and a cup of coffee,' which I did.

Up like a shot he was, and nimble with it, and across the street to a liquor store, where he bought a bottle of 'Red Biddy', finishing the whole lot in practically one go. He said nothing, but offered me the drop, but dear God, even if I was on the drink, I would hope to find ways and means of getting something better than this.

Every country has got its Boweryites. It's a funny thing, but everybody who goes to France for a couple of weeks, seems to get the idea that the French are a very abstemious race. They forget the fact that forty-eight thousand people die there from alcoholism every year.

I was on a farm once in France, and although admittedly they drank plenty of wine, the men also drank a type of *pastis* which they made from the grape skins after the juice had been pressed out of them, and they mixed it with a substance which they must have got from round the back of the chemist's shop. It would be better used for cleaning horses' hooves. But it was an abominable mixture and extremely potent with it.

Most people look upon the English as being a very sober race, but I know a lot of them who, I would say, have a stiff upper lip mostly because they are 'stiff' twenty-four hours a day.

I left my alcoholic friend, and looking for something more cheerful, I went in to see *Sammy's Bowery Follies*, where, someone told me, 'bums and swells mingle together'.

The devil take the begrudgers; I do not flatter myself that I am either of these. But I do consider myself fortunate for having seen the show. It was extremely entertaining and I did not expect to see anything so cheerful on the Bowery. I think Sammy must have hired former vaudevillians for the cabaret because they were not exactly, shall I say, 'young pro's'. But they did the best they could under difficult circumstances. As Oscar Wilde wisely remarked: 'The soul is born old but grows young. That is the comedy of life. The body is born young and grows old. That's life's tragedy.'

On one of the walls in the place was a notice: 'The foolish and wicked practice of profane swearing is a vice so low and mean that every person of sense and character despises it.'

'I haven't opened my bloody mouth,' I said to a friend of mine. I was sitting with a cartoonist of the New York *Post*, and with Freddie Boland, an Irishman, who was President of the United Nations at the time, and Tim Costello was with us too. Poor Tim – the Lord have mercy on him – but he nearly went mad if you pronounced his name in one way, because it sounded like the name of a gentleman whom the government was always trying to deport from the United States for not being a very choice character.

However, a reporter from an Irish-American paper came over and wanted to interview me on my impressions of life in the Bowery. Now I have nothing against Irish papers in New York and I have been reading the *Irish World* regularly since childhood, because an uncle of mine living there used to send it home to us.

It is owned by Miss Ford, a descendant of Patrick Ford, who was described in the House of Commons as the greatest enemy the British Empire ever had. This was in the time of Parnell and during the war against the landlords in Ireland. The circulation of the *Irish World* in those days was over a million copies, and it is still a very good paper, and a paper I respect.

'I'm sorry,' I said to this reporter, 'but I have been giving interviews all day and I don't feel in the humour for giving any more just at the moment. If you want to set one up, speak to my press agent, Abner Klipstein, who handles these kind of things for me.'

And I thought the man was going to do himself serious damage.

'Look here,' he shouted. 'We made you and we can break you.'

'Who, in the name of bejasus, are you?' I said. 'What newspaper are you from anyway?'

So he told me he was from the 'Irish Corned Beef Journal' or something. Anyway it was a weekly paper which denounced emigration from Ireland in its editorials, and then carried an advertisement from the proprietor announcing how his travel agency would bring over your husband, your wife, your son, your daughter, your granny and any old aunt, and would fix up about visas and all to that effect. At a fee of course.

'In that case,' I said to him, speaking in Irish, 'we had better speak in Irish, because I do not speak American all that well.'

After a few minutes, he left.

'Don't mind that fellow,' Tim said. 'The Chinese have a better newspaper below in Mott Street, only I can't read it because it is printed sideways.'

'Where's Mott Street?' I asked.

'Oh, it's in Chinatown, down past the Bowery. And if you haven't been to Chinatown, it is well worth a visit for the restaurants alone. They are extremely good.'

Now for one *restaurateur* to say that about another *restaurateur*, is quite a compliment.

My wife is very fond of Chinese food and, to a certain extent, I like the novelty of it. I remember I was in 'Johnny Chan's' in San Francisco, and at the end of the meal we were given a wonderful drink called 'Almond Eye,' which is a white liquid and most palatable. For the sake of the 'Almond Eye,' I was willing to go to Chinatown and eat all the birds' nests from there to Hong Kong.

Frank Hogan, the District Attorney, told me that in Chinatown there is a very low juvenile delinquency rate and he attributed this to the influence of their Chinese ancestors.

'Damn it,' I replied, 'their ancestors are mostly dead.'

'Yes,' he said, 'but they have a tremendous spirit of family kinship and they do seem able to control their teenagers in a way which is far better than most parents.'

To be sure the kids on the streets were more polite than any teenagers I've seen the world over, and they stepped off the pavements for us to go past and nodded and smiled, and some of them even spoke to us. As far as a superficial view could carry me, I found it quite true to say that the Chinese in Chinatown, whether young or old, were a very highly civilized and gentle people.

I saw plenty of action though, in the sense that there was plenty of

good food and a fair amount of drinking 'Almond Eye', and I saw
the boys and girls on the streets enjoying themselves. I also passed a
dance hall where they seemed to be having great fun.

The proprietor of one Chinese restaurant told me that these children could speak pure American on the street and automatically change
to their own Chinese dialect the moment they came into the house.

The shops there are beautiful too, and I'd say that if you wouldn't
be minding sharkfin soup for the rest of your life, Chinatown would
be a tolerable place in which to live.

I believe many, many years ago, there were Chinese brothels in
New York. Well, I suppose there were brothels then for every
nationality. My own native city, despite the fact that it is one of the
most religious cities on the face of the earth, had, up until 1913, what
was called 'a tolerated quarter', and a pretty big one it was too.
James Joyce described it in *Ulysses* as 'Night-town'. And the brothels
were licensed and the prostitution was organized in the district by
Prince Max of Battenburg, an ancestor of the Duke of Edinburgh.

However, Chinatown is a very respectable area nowadays, but I
heard tell that in the tougher times, one lady used to advertise: 'Two
bitty, seeie; Four bitty, feelie; Six bitty, doie.'

This, of course, was all in the faraway past.

BOWERY BAR

COMMANDER-IN-CHIEF

FRANKIE - Bowery type

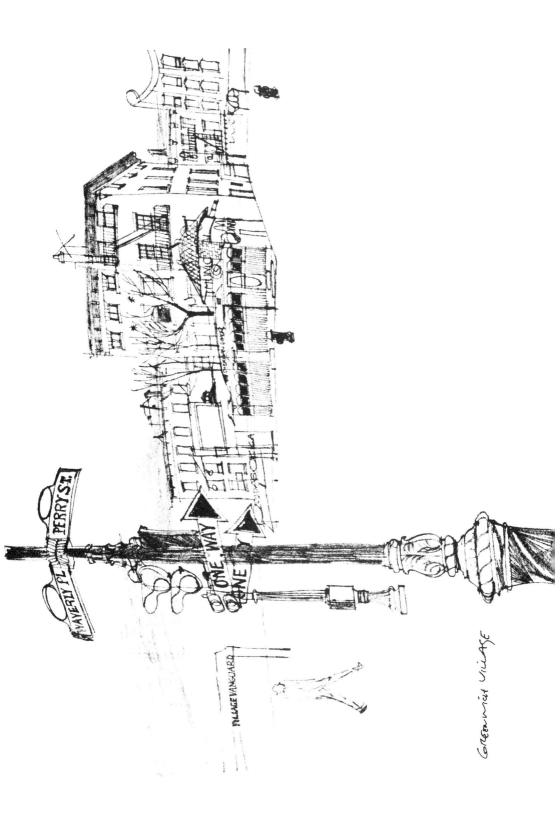

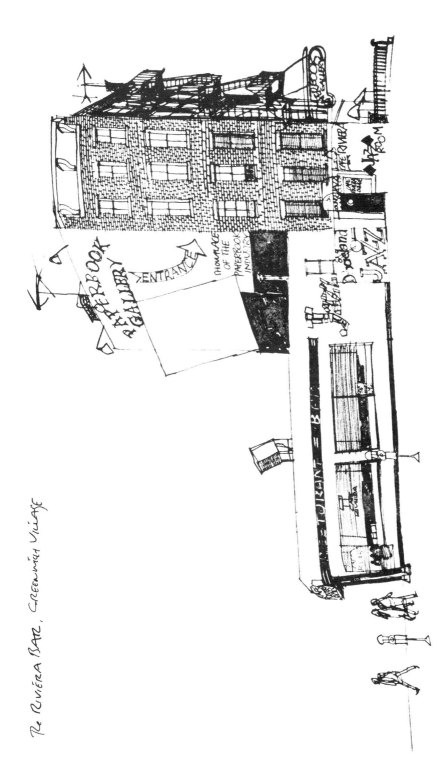

The Riviera Bar, Greenwich Village

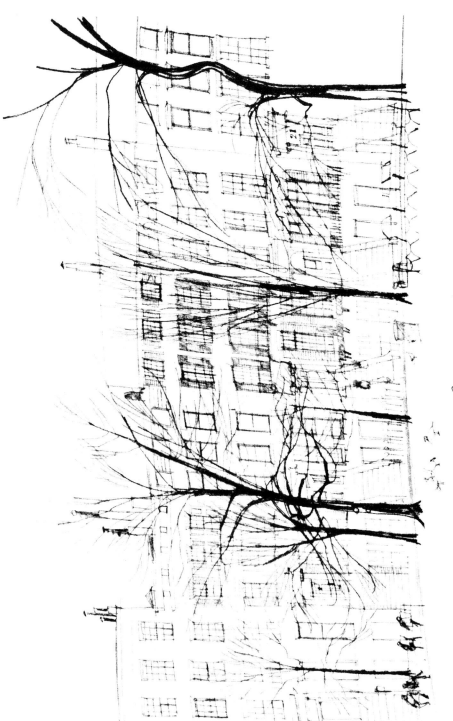

The Georgian Houses of WASHINGTON SQUARE, Greenwich VILLAGE

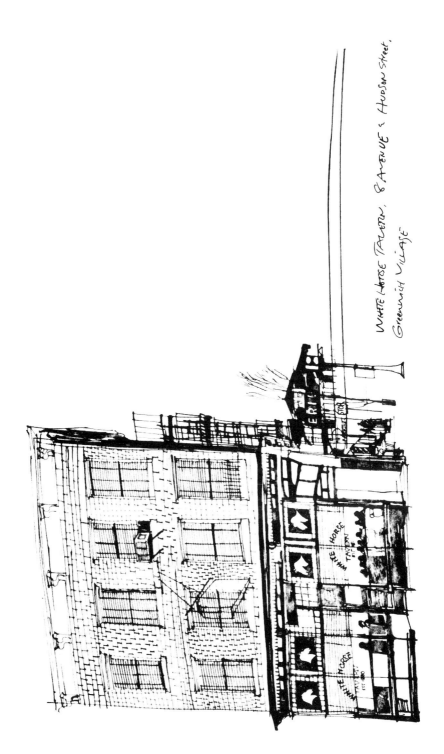

WHITE HORSE TAVERN, 8 AVENUE & HUDSON STREET.
GREENWICH VILLAGE

SAMMY'S BOWERY FOLLIES

Sammy's Bowery Follies

Re BOWERY

CHINATOWN

MAN HATTAN FROM STATEN ISLAND

Give my regards
to Staten Island

The cheapest voyage you can have in the world is from New York City to Staten Island, which costs five cents. I have an uncle, by the name of Jimmy Kearney, living there and he has been in America since after the First World War.

And he enjoys Staten Island to such an extent that he has only been home to Ireland once during this time. In fact he very rarely leaves his house, except to go to work.

When I first came to New York, I rang up my Aunt Kathleen and asked her where I would find my Uncle Jimmy.

'Oh,' she said, 'he works at Pine Street, off Wall Street, in the Chase Manhattan Bank.'

'Would you mind telling me,' I said, 'on what floor I will find him, for the buildings here are larger than any other place I was ever in?'

'Your Uncle Jimmy is on every floor.'

'God bless us and save us,' said I, 'he must be the bank's vice-president.'

'No,' she said, 'he's the elevator man.'

But I do not think that my uncle would have come back to Ireland at all, if the BBC had not flown him home for a television show on my father's life called, *This Is Your Life*.

But Uncle Jimmy always sent us home a dollar or two, which I remember changing in the post office across the street. Even during the depression in America, he managed to send us some money, because there was a depression everywhere, the likes of which I hope we will never see again.

I also hope, incidentally, that we won't see the H-bomb. The only thing is, that the suffering from the H-bomb will not last as long as the suffering during the depression.

The Irish in America are always faithful to what they describe as 'the old country', and although we have a great affection for America, we do not call it that.

I do not expect everyone to love the Irish – I don't expect anyone to love everyone anywhere – but perhaps some of the people in the United States who do not like us, though I did not meet any, might suggest that our affection for their country generally, is a question of cupboard love.

At this point I may say, however, that the Republic of Ireland does not get, officially, any of the handouts that the rest of the world seems to be getting from America. As a matter of fact, it is estimated that a working man pays out roughly an English pound, or two dollars and eighty cents, from his wages every week, for distribution to other nations. At the same time, the United Nations states that the Republic of Ireland is the best-fed nation in the entire world.

However, I went over to Staten Island on this five-cent ferry, which is a marvellous deal. The only thing is, sadly enough, that like a great many other places, you cannot swim in the Hudson or in the East Side River any more. Nor can you in the Liffey, nor in the lower reaches of the Thames in London, nor even in the Seine. And I happen to like swimming round the docks, because I learned to swim in the Dublin docks.

To tell the honest truth, the architecture on Staten Island did not particularly impress me, but I did understand the reason why my uncle had only stopped five days in Ireland on his free trip. I would think the bloody cold nearly killed him, for his house is centrally heated and is a comfortable working-class family home.

But he had acquired some extraordinary American habits, and one of them was that he would not leave his job at the bank to come out for a drink during working hours. Now I have never heard of such a heresy before in my life, particularly when his immediate boss was a Dublin Jew.

So I invited him out to lunch and I nearly dropped dead because he drank milk with his food. He had acquired a kind of horror of drink.

And he could not get on that ferry fast enough for to get back to Staten Island. Now I am not knocking Staten Island, but it's not exactly, shall I say, Monte Carlo, at least as far as I could see. But I suppose if a person happens to come from a particular area, like any other city in the world, well that's their spot.

I asked my uncle how often he had been over to Manhattan of an evening and he told me he had not been there since the first night of my play, *The Hostage*.

'What do I want to go to Manhattan for?' he said. 'There is everything in the world I want on Staten Island.'

Well, when the late Archbishop Mannix first arrived in Sydney, an Australian docker, who was carrying his luggage, dropped a very heavy suitcase on his own toe. And he uttered some foul language that an archbishop would not normally be hearing.

'Oh, bloody hell,' the docker said.

But the Archbishop wasn't a bit knocked out. 'That's right,' he said. 'Every man for his own country.'

And this I have to say about my relations' loyalty to Staten Island.

But both my uncle and my aunt were at the first-night party of *The Hostage* and we went to Downey's restaurant. Lauren Bacall was in the company, and Jason Robards, Jr. and Jackie Gleason.

'Come on,' Jackie said to me, 'let's talk Irish.'

'Where the hell did you learn Irish?' I asked him.

'Oh, I can count up to ten,' he said.

So I asked him in Irish, 'How are you, Jackie?'

'One, two, three, four,' he replied.

Presently Freddie Boland of the Irish Delegation to the United Nations joined us. He is an old friend of mine, as indeed are all his family. His wife incidentally is a painter, and we worked together as painters one time, except she was painting murals and I was painting the wall, back home in Dublin.

This night, Freddie Boland had just come from the United Nations, where they were electing a new president.

'Your show went well, I see,' he said. 'I've read the reviews. Come to that, my own show went well. I was elected President of the United Nations.'

I introduced my uncle and aunt to him and they congratulated him, but I am afraid they were really more interested in Jackie Gleason. They wanted to tell my little cousin Margaret that they had spoken to Jackie Gleason, which apparently was like having an audience with the Pope.

Now I have a great affection for my cousin, Margaret, because she is the youngest of my generation, but she would not leave the goddam television off. Fortunately it was in another room in the house, where she could watch it with some friends of hers.

The two things that the American teenage girl appears to worship have both, oddly enough, Greek names: the telephone and television. I think, without any disrespect to the Greek Orthodox Church, that this should be their religion, instead of Roman Catholicism, because nobody has ever heard of Romanvision or Romanphone. But you wouldn't be in a house with a young American girl for very long without being most conscious of them both.

Now I do not like to knock television, because to a certain extent, I make my living by it. But it would put years on you, watching the damn thing day and night.

Everybody on Staten Island seemed to have a car, except me. I do not know how to drive. I'm not that much of a fool. Perhaps I am, for I would probably have the whole road to myself, after a while. But I wouldn't wish it on the lamp-posts and the trees and the hedges. As long as there are taxis – and the two best taxi towns in the world are New York and London – I don't want to drive a car.

While I was having tea with my uncle and aunt – and it was real tea, not out of those goddam bags – my eldest first cousin drove over from further up the Island, for to meet me. He is a very good-looking boy of about twenty-two summers, and he is married to an Italian girl and they have a beautiful Italian baby or an Irish-Italian baby or a New York baby.

Actually, I suppose she is a Staten Island baby, because the Staten

Street Scene on Staten Island

Islanders are rather prone to point out that they are not from Manhattan.

Jimmy brought a kid called Steve with him, who was the first New Yorker that I had met, and also the only one that I know who does not claim any racial affiliations outside of Staten Island. He did not even claim any on Manhattan Island, or Queen's Island, or the Bronx, for the matter of that. He had been at school with Jimmy Junior and had just emerged from the army.

Now Jimmy didn't like being called Junior very much, because naturally he felt that although his father was Jimmy Kearney, he too, was also Jimmy Kearney. And I've yet to meet a boy in America who wanted to be called Junior.

'Tomorrow night,' young Jimmy said, 'I'll drive you up to my house, and you'll meet my wife and my baby and I will show you my tank of tropical fish.'

He had a wonderful aquarium like my friend George Kleinsinger in the Hotel Chelsea, except that it wasn't quite so elaborate, as there is more space in the Hotel Chelsea than there is in the whole of Staten Island.

The myth of the English and the Irish eating the face off each other in New York, is not entirely true.

We were all going out to dinner and my aunt asked me if we might bring along Mrs. Marino.

'She is a good neighbour of ours, and she is one of our own,' she said.

'No doubt,' I said, 'you mean that she's a Catholic?' Not, I hasten to add, that I am a very good advertisement for the Catholic faith.

'A Catholic?' my Aunt Kathleen replied. 'Mrs. Marino hates them, except that she likes us.'

'I suppose you mean that she is an Italian, then?' I said.

'Goodness me, no. She hates them too. Her former husband was an Italian.'

'In the name of God,' I said, 'how do you mean, "she's one of our own?"'

'Ah,' she said, 'Mrs. Marino comes from Birmingham. Birmingham in England, I mean.'

Now I do not wish to take any custom away from Jim Downey or Vincent Sardi, or from my good friend Jack Lipsett who owns a restaurant called the Monte Rosa on Forty-eighth Street. It is an Italian restaurant, with Spanish waiters, a Jewish proprietor and a largely Irish clientele, and is one of the most interesting places I was ever in in my life. It is also a bit of a madhouse, but that's beside the point.

However, I would not want to do any of these people out of a crust, but I discovered a restaurant on Staten Island, where I had the most excellent meal which cost about twenty-five per cent of what it would have cost on Manhattan. And you have to allow for the terrible expense of getting from Manhattan to Staten Island, which is five cents.

In New York, every restaurant is either Italian, Chinese, Irish, Hebrew or even English. There is an English restaurant called Keen's which, I understand, is patronized by Eamon De Valera, but I think he only goes there for the tea. I suppose the Americans have got a restaurant of their own, but I never saw one.

Anyway, this one on Staten Island is called Henny's Steak House, though funnily enough the Italian-American proprietor serves mainly Italian food. And doing the Broadway big shot, the sophisticate who had been to Paris, I asked for champagne. It is a drink which I am extremely fond of and a drink which I flatter myself I know a little about. I have heard of Veuve Clicquot, and Pommery and Heidsieck, but the proprietor of this restaurant brought me a bottle of champagne which I had never heard of.

'I don't know this one,' I told him. 'What part of France does it come from?'

'It comes from upstate, in New York,' he said. It was all right, I can tell you, and the food was marvellous.

We had a very good party and we sang Irish songs. Real Irish songs, for sometimes I have heard Irish songs in America that you would never be hearing in Ireland. One time I met a New Yorker who told me that the Irish National Anthem was a song called: 'Who put the Overalls in Mrs. Murphy's Chowder?'

In actual fact, the Irish National Anthem was written by my mother's brother, Peadar Kearney, who was also the brother of Uncle Jimmy living on Staten Island. His aunt, Mary Kearney, fled from her father's farm in the County Meath to Madison Avenue, nearly eighty years ago.

Here are letters written to John Kearney, my mother's father, from his sister and brother, my Great-aunt Mary and my Great-uncle Patrick.

FROM PATRICK KEARNEY

Cabin Creek,
Johnson Co.,
Arkansas, U.S. January 6th, 1885

My dear brother,

I received your welcome letter today. I am glad to hear you and Katie and family are well, also Hugh and Mary. I am not very well as I am writing this. I am glad to hear you are getting on so well in business. I want you to send me Tom's address in St. Louis if you have it. St. Louis is a big city, so it would be hard for me to find him out if I did not know the street he lives in. I would like to hear from him.

Well, dear John, I will go to Dublin next summer, about July, please God, if I can, no matter what happens. That is if you give me or if I can get work for a while. Our pay was cut to $1.00 a day. I pay $5.00 a month for board and one dollar for washing. My boss is a Tipperary man and his wife is from Co. Louth: she is out here since she was a girl. There is a man here named James Thornton from Co. Louth: he knows where Talunstown and Dunleer are; he knows Lord Louth . . . A man here from Newbridge also. They are about the only company I have, as the natives here are a poor, ignorant, half-starved, famished lot, with nothing to eat but corn meat and fat pork. You may talk about houses in Ireland, but I never saw half as bad houses as there are here.

But the people here are too lazy to go to work, so you see it is their own fault. I get good board but pay dear for it. I hope you had a merry Christmas and a happy New Year. As for me, only for the few men I had with me, it would have been very lonesome. I sent you a paper three weeks ago; it is hard to get papers here but I will send you one in a day or two. Hoping to hear from you soon. Remember me to all friends, with much love to you and Katie, Peter (Peadar) and Margaret,

I remain your loving brother,

Patrick Kearney

FROM MARY KEARNEY

Southampton, Long Island,
New York. September 9th, 1889

My dear brother,
   I received a letter from Thomas [another brother who had also emigrated to the United States] and Pat. Thomas sent me his picture; it is taken on tin, so I don't care to send it to you. He has got to be a fine boy. He is very like you and writes just like you when you were in Curragh Camp. I think Thomas is doing well, although he meets ups and downs.
   Pat wrote rather a lonely letter. He said he would like to go to Dublin. I would like if he would go to see you next summer. He was nearly dying some months ago. He is a thousand miles from Tom. I want you to write to them and I will send you their addresses. Tom will leave there in four weeks; Pat wants him to go to Washington for the winter.
   I can't tell you how good I feel to hear of them being alive. I am writing to Pat and will give him your address. You will have this letter before Pat has mine, so write to him and it will keep him from being lonely. You may have a letter from Thomas before Pat. Tell Hugh they were asking for him. I am watching his picture every day. With fondest love to all, believe me, your affectionate sister.

                         Mary Kearney   Write soon.

FROM PATRICK KEARNEY

Fairhaven,
Whatcomco,
Washington, U.S.A. 21st December, 1890

My dear brother John,
   I take the pleasure of writing these few lines hoping you, wife and family are well. I received *Weekly Freeman* and also the three song ballads you sent. I just worked $6\frac{1}{2}$ days after I sent you the last letter. The Company got done and paid off every man, I have not done anything since. Work is done until Spring, and that is the great trouble in America, work six months in the year, the other six lay idle. The Union Pacific Railway Co. are building 20 miles of new road

about 200 miles from here, and from the latest reports in the newspaper they have closed down between three and four thousand men. Well, they all flock to the towns and city.

There is nothing doing, and anything that may be going, there are so many to look for it. The fact is there are too many emigrants of all classes coming here who don't understand a word of English and will work for mere nothing, and other men have to compete in order to live. I have done a good deal of running around in America seeking the best place, but all to my sorrow I have lost by it. The American country is gone. If a man today in America, from the Atlantic to the Pacific, doesn't belong to a secret order or society, such as the Odd Fellows, the Masons and numerous others, he can get nothing. I am sorry to say there are several Irishmen turning over every day. I intend to buy some business, such as keeping a saloon, or, as it is called in Ireland, a public house. If I have any chance of making money next Summer, I am going to buy something. If people leave Ireland to come to America to make money, they will be badly left if they depend on the land work, because what they earn in Summer, they eat in Winter. I have tried as hard as anybody. It is a great pity to see all the young Irishmen going to the bad in America. They come here from the old country, where they had places as clerks, store or shop keepers, living a good life – thinking they can do better. But they are mistaken; they think they can't do hard work; well, they have to come to it or become tramps; rather than hard work some become highway robbers and thieves of all kinds. I see the Dublin men are the worst. Them that do come in from their work in some remote place in the logging camps or country roads after two or three months having $10 or $15. Just as they reach town, they go into the saloon, drinking from bad to worse, don't care about the Church or anything, get ashamed of themselves, never write to their people. Some get enough money and may go back to Ireland all broken down. Of course a steady man is much better off in America than Ireland under her present conditions. But what is a few pounds to a body when they run such a chance of losing their good health, the main part of life?

This town is two years old and has a population of about 6,000 people. It is a new country and rains six months of the year, and, of course, the earth is always damp. Wood is plentiful here. The new streets that have been made are planted instead of paved. 2 and 3 inch boards, side walks wood, and in making these streets, the doctors say, have caused a great deal of sickness: over a hundred people died here last Summer and Autumn. Of course there is not a word about this; they know it would keep settlers from coming here.

I have been alright all the Summer. I had a bottle of medicine, thank God. I had a letter from Mary; she had some of her teeth pulled out. I was sorry to hear of her trouble.

I often think I am long enough in this country to go to Ireland again, but what is the use of thinking? I should not attempt to do so without a few hundred pounds. I received the old ancient picture you sent me and I must say you are a fine hand at drawing the harp and wolf dog and America. Flag is well done. I hope to live and see the old place.

The Parnell affair is the main talk among the sensible and settled class. Irishmen all over America have taken many dollars out of Envoy's (Parnell's) pocket, which he should have got had this unfortunate trouble not occurred. The Torys could not beat him in his great case two years ago (the Pigott forgeries) and unfortunately succeeded in the O'Shea Case in breaking up the Liberal Party; and as the papers say, they are laughing up their sleeves at the Irish Party. Well, if it is a fact it is something disgraceful to all Ireland, that someone threw time into Parnell's lap. And the great or terrible club fighting in Tipperary with the Parnell and McCarthy cliques is most disgraceful and causes Irishmen to lose the sympathy of America. It would be better for Parnell to resign at once than to have trouble. He will always be regarded by America as a great leader.

Still, I hope you will have a merry Christmas and a happy New Year. Do not forget brother Hugh; please God, when Summer turns up I will see that you are paid for your trouble. There is not much use in saying much about him, just content yourself that people in Ireland don't trouble him. It is safe for me to say he is not making a fortune and it's better he stayed in Ireland; but we must hope he is doing well.

Patrick Kearney

FROM MARY KEARNEY

323 *Madison Avenue,*
New York City. October 24th, '92

My dear brother,

Your fond letter I received a week ago. Glad to hear all are well. I am real well. I had some trouble looking for work, it is hard to get here at present. About poor Pat, he is in hospital in California, my heart is sore thinking of him far away from us all. I fear we shall lose him. Thomas had a letter from you. It was in the post a long time. He had to leave there to get work elsewhere. If Pat would stay here near to town or write to you or to me, he would be better off. The doctor said he can leave the hospital in a month. I am sorry to see you had to pay on the papers, and about coming to this country, do as you please, you have your chance to make a living, but believe me you will find a change.

It would be better to sell them houses than to be worrying your mind with them. I have no money to send you as I have to help Pat this Winter. See if Mr. McGuinness would help you. Peter (Peadar) is a nice writer, he will soon be able to write to me. Tell Hugh about me and poor Pat. Pray for him. I send my love to you and all the children.

Your affectionate sister,
(Unsigned)

FROM MARY KEARNEY

Undated.

My dear brother,

Glad to hear all are well. I am much better in health this Winter than I have been for some time, thank God. Well, we have terrible snow storms here, never so bad in 18 years, and the terrible cold is something awful on the poor. You may think Dublin or parts of Ireland bad, but the poverty of this city is something you could not believe. All the poorer classes are idle, no work for men, it is good for girls. Pat did not find any work, he may get some in March and you see a man doesn't care to write when he is idle. Thomas did not work only for two years, only odd jobs; last Summer he went to Canada and worked for only three months. Poor fellow he gets it hard. I tell you this country is no good, only for the rich. Pat did not say much about Ireland, but as he has been in this country so many years, he could not live in Ireland any more. But I think he might have more clothes with him and not come to see me so shabby. I don't want to see anyone unless they are looking respectable and clothes are so cheap in Dublin, 10 dollars would get him a nice suit of clothes. If you had to help him, I would have paid you. I leave here on 1st. April as the family goes to England for six months, so I will have a letter if you write to me as soon as you get this. I will go to the country this Summer. With fond love to all, believe me,

Your fond sister,
M. Kearney

These letters are included in the life of Peadar Kearney, author of 'The Soldier's Song', Ireland's National Anthem, by Seamus de Burca, my cousin, whom I would like to thank for allowing me to reprint them.

My father's people did not go to America because they thought it was a land for country people, but he has connections with the United States. His dear friend, Jack Basnett, a sailor, was drowned in the East River forty years ago, and I had a show on Broadway.

So between Broadway plays and babies and banks and tropical fish, not to mention my mother's cousin and early sweetheart, Pat MacGuinness, chief philosopher of Kearney's saloon on Third Avenue, my mother's people have lived happily, not ever after, for it is not over yet, but have lived happily most of the time in America, and with the help of God and varied, they will continue to do so.

And the same to you and yours.

Index

Abbey Theatre, 42
Alex, Monsieur, 84
Algonquin Hotel, 1, 22–4, 82, 122
American Supreme Court, 25–6
Aqueduct Race Track, 45
Archie and Mehitabel, 79

Baby Grand Club, 96
Bacall, Lauren, 143
Baldwin, Jimmy, 39
Bankhead, Tallulah, 80
Bar Mitzvah, 20–4
Bard, Mr., 78
Bard, Stanley, 78
Battenburg, Prince Max of, 129
BBC, 42, 115, 141
Beach, Sylvia, 116–17
Beat Generation, the, 119
Beckett, Samuel, 120
Behan, Beatrice, 12–13, 27, 42, 84, 89
Belmont Racetrack, 45
Bennett, Bob, 24
Berman, Shelley, 20
Betjeman, John, 80
Black Muslims, 94
Blacks, The, 115
'Blue Angel', 19–20

Boland, Freddie, 127, 144
Boucicault, Dion, 20
Boulevard St. Germain, 94, 118
Boulton, Agnes, 78
Bowery, the, 122–9
Brasserie, 27
Braque, Georges, 28
Briscoe, Robert, 62
Broadway, 12, 18, 20, 24, 42–6, 50, 58, 84, 87, 89, 120, 125, 147, 153
Bronx, 146
Bronx Zoo, 97–8
Brooklyn, 88, 115, 122
Brooklyn Heights, 114
Brooks Brothers, 22
Bruskin, Perry, 115
Bryn Mawr College, 22

Canadian Broadcasting Corporation, 16
Candida (see Lycett-Green)
Capone, Al, 79
Cashel Byron's Profession, 47
Cearnaich, Conal, 28
Central Park, 97
Champs-Elysées, 39
Chan, Johnny, 128
Channel Islands, 123

Chaplin, Oona (*née* O'Neill), 78
Chase Manhattan Bank, 141
'Chateaubriand', the, 84
Chayefsky, Paddy, 24
Cherry Grove, 90–2
Chinatown, 114, 128–9
'Chumley's', 114
Cinque Georges, 124
'Circle in the Square, The', 115
Claridges, 124
Cohan, George Michael, 42
Collins, Michael, 115
Columbia Broadcasting System, 49
Coney Island, 88–9
Connection, The, 115
Connolly, Cyril, 16
Costello, Mrs., 60
'Costello's', 56–60
Costello, Tim, 56–60, 79, 127–8
Costello, Joe, 56

Daly, Mr., 50
David, Jacques Louis, 14
Davies, Arthur B., 78
de Burca, Seamus, 152
Dempsey, Jack, 46
De Valera, Eamon, 147
'Douanier Le', 29
Douglas, William O., 25
Downey, Jim, 45, 147
Downey's restaurant, 27, 44–5, 143
Duffy, Father, 12, 44

Edinburgh, Duke of, 129
Egan, Colonel Eddie, 47
Eiffel, Gustave, 40–1
Eiffel Tower, 40
Emmet, Robert, 52
Emmet, Thomas Addis, 52
Empire State Building, 56
England, Bishop, 52
Eton, 26
Exiles, 117

Farrell, James T., 78
Fields, Frank, 96–7

Fire Island, 88–9
Fitzgerald, Scott, 117
Flaherty, Robert, 78
Flynn, Mrs. Elizabeth Gurley, 79
Ford, Miss, 127
Ford, Patrick, 127
'Four Seasons', 27
Fox, Father Tom, 120
Francis, Arlene, 49
Fulton Fish Market, 53–4

Gallagher, Johnnie, 60
Garfinkle, Jeannie, 82
Garfinkle, Willie, 82–4
Geis, Bernard, 84
Gelber, Jack, 115
Genet, Jean, 115
Ginevan, Eddie, 45
Ginsberg, Allen, 118
'Give My Regards to Broadway', 42
Gladstone, William Ewart, 78
Gleason, Jackie, 143–4
Gordon, 78
Gordon, Max, 19
Greenwich Village, 113–16, 118
'Guernica', 30

Harding, Gilbert, 16
Harlem, 92, 96, 114
Harlow, Jean, 62
Harriman, Governor, 27–8
Harrow, 26
Harvard, 46–7
Hemingway, Ernest, 58, 117–18
Henny's Steak House, 147
Henry, O., 78
Hoffer, Bernie, 13
Hogan, Frank S., 13–14, 16, 128
Hogarth, Paul, 60
Hollywood, 26, 47
Hospitals, 16
Hostage, The, 12, 39, 46, 96, 115, 143
Hotel Chelsea, 77–80, 84–6, 122, 146
Howe, Admiral Lord, 50
Howl, 118
Hurley Brothers and Daly, 50

Hurleys, the 50
Hyde Park, 123

Importance of Being Oscar, The, 120
Irish Club, 97
Irish World, 127

Jeffs, Rae, 84
Jimmy (see Kearney)
Jimmy Junior (see Kearney)
'Jimmy Glennon's', 60
Johnson, Dr., 120
Joyce, James, 27, 78, 117, 123, 129

Kathleen (see Kearney)
Kearney, Jimmy, 141–2, 146, 148
Kearney Jr., Jimmy, 146
Kearney, John, 148
Kearney, Kathleen, 64, 141, 146
Kearney, Mary, 148
Kearney, Great-uncle Patrick, 148
Kearney, Peadar, 147, 152
Kearney's Saloon, 64–5, 153
Keen's, 147
Kelly, Walt, 58
Kennedy Airport, 35
Kennedy, President, 28
Kernoff, Harry, 19
Kerouac, Jack, 118–19
Kerr, Walter, 46
Kilcreene Lodge, 14
Kinsey, Doctor, 26
Kleinsinger, George, 79–80, 98, 146
Kline, Franz, 30, 114
Klipstein, Abner, 127

Larkin, Jim, 54
Lipsett, Jack, 147
London, 12
Long Island railroad, 89
'Lost Generation', the, 119
Lycett-Green, Candida (*née* Betjeman), 80–2
Lyons, Leonard, 20, 26–7, 124

McCarthy, Senator, 79
McCormick, Tommy, 60–1
McGlory, Kevin, 62

MacGuinness, Miss, 65
MacGuinness, Patrick, 64–5, 153
MacLiammoir, Michael, 120
MacNeven, William, 52
McNulty, 58
McSorley, 56
McSorley's Old Ale House, 53–4
Mailer, Norman, 39, 114
Manhattan, 13, 41–2, 115, 143, 146–7
Mannix, Archbishop, 143
'Ma O'Brien's', 60
Marquis, Don, 79
Martini Building, 39
Marty, 24
Masters, Edgar Lee, 78
Mencken, H. L., 58, 114
Merman, Ethel, 24
Metropole, The, 42
Miller, Arthur, 78
Monte Rosa, 147
Mott Street, 128
Museum of Modern Art, 30

Naked and the Dead, The, 39
National Broadcasting Company, 49–50
New York Boxing Commission, 47
New York Harbour, 40–1
New York Herald-Tribune, 46
New York Post, 20, 58, 127
New York Public Library, 50
New York Reporters Association, 48
New York Stock Exchange, 50, 97
New York Times, the, 46
'Night-town', 129

Oasis Saloon, 82–4
O. Henry's Steak House, 114
O'Neill, Eugene Gladstone, 78
O'Neill James, 79
O'Neill, Shane, 78
'One Sheridan Square', 115
O'Shea, Kitty, 78
O'Sullivan, Séan, 19
'Over There', 42

Paar, Jack, 49
Paris, 39, 116–19, 147

Paris Theatre Society, 39
Parnell, 78, 127
Pennsylvania Station, 89
People, 77
Philadelphia, 22
Phoenix Park, 98, 124
Picasso, Pablo, 27, 30
Piccadilly, 42
Pines Boatel, The, 89
'P. J. Clarke's', 62
'Pogo', 58
Pravda, 47
President of the United Nations, 144

Quare Fellow, The, 115
Quintero, Jose, 115

Rabelais, François, 84
R.C.A., 56
Rhys, Keidrych, 77
Richard's Cork Leg, 117
'Ricky's', 114
Roaring Twenties Club, 26
Robards Jr., Jason, 143
Rockefeller Center, 50
Rogers, Father Herbert, 20
Roosevelt, Franklin D., 79
Rousseau, Henri, 29
Royal Dublin Society's Dog Show, 18
Runyon, Damon, 48
Russell, Nipsey, 96

St. Anthony's Church, 114
St. George Hotel, 88
Saint Nicholas Avenue, 96
Saint Nicholas Terrace, 92
Saint Patrick, 96
Saint Patrick's Cathedral, 44
Saint Patrick's Day, 18–20, 52, 65, 114, 120
St. Paul's Chapel, 50, 52
Saints and Sinners Club, 47
Sammy's Bowery Follies, 126
San Gennaro, 114
San Gennaro, Feast of, 114
Sardi, Vincent, 27, 44–6, 147
Savoy Ballroom, 92
Schrafft's restaurants, 84

Seal, Elizabeth, 48
Sexual Behaviour in the Human Male, 26
Shakespeare, 46–7, 123
Shaw, Bernard, 47
Sheridan, Captain, 41
'Silver Rail', the, 84–6
Sinn Fein, 94
'Six Butchers of Broadway' the, 45
Sloan, John, 54, 78
Smith, Al, 54
Smithwick, Walter, 14
Soho, 118
'Soldier's Song, The', 152
Statue of Liberty, 40–1
'Stefan's', 114
Stein, Gertrude, 117–18
Studs Lonigan, 78

Taubman Howard, 46
Tenth Man, The, 24
Theatre de l'Œuvre, 117
Théâtre des Nations, 39
Thomas, Caitlin, 77
Thomas, Dylan, 77–8, 114
Thompson, Dorothy, 79
Thurber, Jim, 58, 119
Time-Life Building, 56
Times Square, 13, 16, 44
Toklas, Alice B., 117–18
Tone, Franchot, 62
Tone, Theobald Wolfe, 62
Toronto, 16
Trinity Church, 50
Tubby the Tuba, 79
Tunney, Gene, 46–7

Ulysses, 117, 129

Vassar College, 18, 22
Versailles, 39
Village, the (see Greenwich Village)

Waldorf Astoria, 124
Walker, Jimmy, 54
Wall Street, 50, 141
Washington, D.C., 26

Washington Arch, 115
Washington, George, 50
Washington Market, 53
Washington Square, 114–15
Waugh, Evelyn, 120
West End, 12
Whipsnade Zoo, 98
'White Horse', the, 114
Wilde, Oscar, 90, 127
Wilder, Thornton, 119
Wolfe, Thomas, 78

Woollcott, Alexander, 58
Wright, Joseph, 50

Yale, 47
Yeats, Jack, 12
Yeats, Jack B., 12
Yeats, William Butler, 12, 28
Yevtushenko, 12
Yom Kippur, 20
Young Men's Christian Association, 86–7
Young Men's Hebrew Association, 87